Consecration in the Chrysalis

Donloyn LeDuff Gadson

Creole Magnolia Publishing

Copyright © 2019 Donloyn LeDuff Gadson
All rights reserved.
Cover art by Donloyn LeDuff Gadson
Visit the author's website at www.Donloyn.com

Scripture quotations marked NKJV are taken from the New King James Version®. Copyright © 1982 by Thomas Nelson. Used by permission. All rights reserved.

Scripture quotations marked NLT are from the Holy Bible, New Living Translation, copyright © 1996, 2004, 2015 by Tyndale House Foundation. Used by permission of Tyndale House Publishers Inc., Carol Stream, Illinois 60188. All rights reserved.

Scripture quotations marked KJV are from the King James Version of the Bible.

Scripture quotations marked NIV are taken from the Holy Bible, New International Version®, NIV®. Copyright © 1973, 1978, 1984, 2011 by Biblica, Inc.™ Used by permission of Zondervan. All rights reserved worldwide. www.zondervan.com The "NIV" and "New International Version" are trademarks registered in the United States Patent and Trademark Office by Biblica, Inc.™

Scripture quotations marked TPT are from The Passion Translation®. Copyright © 2017, 2018 by Passion & Fire Ministries, Inc. Used by permission. All rights reserved. ThePassionTranslation.com.

Scripture quotations marked CEB are taken from the Common English Bible® Copyright © 2010, 2011 by Common English Bible,™ Used by permission. All rights reserved worldwide, The "CEB" and "Common English Bible" trademarks are registered in the United States Patent and Trademark Office by Common English Bible. Use of either trademark requires the permission of Common English Bible.

Scripture quotations marked ESV are from the ESV® Bible (The Holy Bible, English Standard Version®), copyright © 2001 by Crossway, a publishing ministry of Good News Publishers. Used by permission. All rights reserved.

2019 Creole Magnolia Publishing Trade Paperback Edition

ISBN: 0-9982952-1-3
ISBN-13: 978-0-9982952-1-3

For every Grace-filled Daughter of God who carries His Glory on her shoulders, His fire in her belly and the Sword of the Spirit in her mouth.

May these words inspire and ignite you.

All Glory to Jehovah God Almighty!

"I beseech you therefore, brethren, by the mercies of God, that you present your bodies a living sacrifice, holy, acceptable to God, which is your reasonable service.

And do not be conformed to this world, but be transformed by the renewing of your mind, that you may prove what is that good and acceptable and perfect will of God."

Romans 12:1-2, NKJV

CONTENTS

BECOMING 1
TO DIE IS TO LIVE 7
CONSECRATION IN THE CHRYSALIS 31
EXHORTATION 41
PREPARATION 53
BEFORE WE BEGIN 69
Preparation Day 1 73
Preparation Day 2 79
Preparation Day 3 85
DEDICATION 91
DISINTEGRATION AND ILLUMINATION 101
ELIMINATION 111
PURIFICATION 119
REVELATION 127
REPLICATION 137
SANCTIFICATION 145
ELEVATION 153
FINAL THOUGHTS 159

DONLOYN LEDUFF GADSON

BECOMING

"'How does one become a butterfly?' she asked pensively. 'You must want to fly so much that you are willing to give up being a caterpillar.' 'You mean to die?' asked Yellow. 'Yes and no,' he answered. 'It looks like you will die, but really you will live.'"
~Trina Paulus, Hope for the Flowers

One of the most intriguing wonders in nature is when a caterpillar becomes a butterfly. The transfiguration of a tiny, furry worm into a graceful, winged creature is both beautiful and amazing. To be changed from an insect that crawls about to one that can fly to amazing heights is a remarkable display of God's majestic power.

When a caterpillar enters its chrysalis, it completely gives way to the process of Becoming. The chrysalis acts as a chamber to facilitate change, growth and coming into being. It serves as a protective compartment dedicated to the caterpillar's transformation, breakthrough and new beginning.

When it is time for a caterpillar to become, its period of gorging on leaves stops. It chooses a safe location on the underside of a twig or branch, and there it deposits a silk pad. It then attaches itself to this silk pad using a hook-like appendage called a cremaster. It wiggles around until it is securely in place. The caterpillar then sheds its skin for the final time, revealing a hard casing called the chrysalis. It is within the chrysalis that an amazing transformation takes place. The process of Becoming is underway. The creature will cease to exist as a caterpillar. Once its transformation is complete, it will breakthrough and commence its new beginning as a butterfly.

The process of Becoming is complicated and beautiful. The desire to become is universal. It transcends all boundaries. It exists in all cultures. But what does it mean to become?

Becoming is defined by dictionary.com as "any process of change; to come, change, or grow to be; to come into being; to develop or grow into; (in the philosophy of Aristotle) any change from the lower level of potentiality to the higher level of actuality."

Becoming is the unlocking and actualization of the hidden potential inside. It's the inserting of a key that reveals a marvelous treasure. It's the inputting of the correct combination of numbers that breaks the seal of a massive vault. Becoming is huge. Yet, the gravity of this grand concept seems to escape most.

Like the caterpillar, we are predisposed and designed for greater. We all climb, struggle, wiggle and strive to become something. But what? What are we trying to become? What does becoming entail? And what does it require? How do we unlock the greater that we carry inside? Very few take the time to explore the depths of these questions.

Here is something important for us to consider. In order to become, we must be willing to give up that which we are. Old beliefs must be set aside. Lifestyles must be abandoned. Ideas, hopes and dreams must fade and vanish. Past thoughts and feelings must be shed and left for dead. In order to become, the former state must pass away. In order to become, we must be willing to die.

Becoming is the ending of one thing and the beginning of the next. It suggests transformation has occurred. It is the battering ram for breakthrough and sounds the alarm for a new beginning. Becoming declares an all-encompassing newness and lays the red carpet for its arrival. Becoming is powerful!

This process of becoming is not exclusive to caterpillars. We, as believers, must also become. And that becoming occurs within the chrysalis—our own spiritual chrysalis. We have been coded and structured for greatness. Deep potential exists in our spiritual DNA. God knew us before we were formed in our mothers' wombs. He knows the thoughts and plans He has for each of us. While we were yet unformed, He wrote and fashioned our days in His book. He rejoices over us in song. The beautiful being God created each of us to become is actualized during the chrysalis experience.

However, in order to become, we must first die.

Prayer for Becoming

Heavenly Father, I humbly, yet boldly, come before You in the Mighty Name of Your Son, My Lord and Savior, Jesus Christ. Father, I ask for wisdom and understanding. Show me who You have designed me to become. Reveal my spiritual DNA. You know the plans you have for me, Father. Share those plans with me. You knew me before I was formed in my mother's womb. Show me who You formed me to be. Show me the "me" I cannot see. Guide me, Father, in this process of Becoming, that I may become all You created me to be for the purpose of bringing You Glory. In Jesus' Mighty and Miraculous Name. Amen.

Write your own personal prayer for Becoming here:

_____

_____

_____

_____

_____

_____

_____

_____

_____

Declarations for Becoming

I declare I will become all that my Heavenly Father has designed me to become.

I declare I am becoming a new creation in Christ.

I declare I have the DNA of Christ.

I declare my new beginning is divinely ordained.

I declare God has written a beautiful story about me in His book, and I will successfully fulfill my role.

I declare God's plans for me are good and will come alive in my life.

I declare The Father will rejoice over me in song as I become who He has called me to be.

I declare I know who I am and who I am to become.

I declare I am fearfully and wonderfully made and am destined for greatness for the glorification of The Father!

I declare I am Becoming!

Write your own declaration for Becoming here:

_____

_____

_____

TO DIE IS TO LIVE

"I have been crucified with Christ; it is no longer I who live, but Christ lives in me; and the life which I now live in the flesh I live by faith in the Son of God, who loved me and gave Himself for me."

~Galatians 2:20, NKJV

The process of Becoming hinges on our ability to die. This, by no means, suggests an actual physical death, but rather a dying to self. It is a crucifying of one's fleshly and sinful ways. It is the killing of all unrighteous ideas, thoughts and desires. It is the process of giving your entire being over to Christ for the advancement of His Kingdom.

But, there is good news! When we die to self, it is not the end. Quite the contrary. It is only the beginning. When we choose to crucify our flesh and die to self as Christ died for us, we can be assured that there will be a resurrection! To die is to live!

Christ came that He might give us life, and life more abundantly (John 10:10). When we give our entire existence over to the Father and His Son Christ Jesus, we are transformed into new creations. We experience breakthroughs and new beginnings that are overflowing with abundance and life. Our Heavenly Father wants us to be willing vessels. He desires to use us in great and magnificent ways. When we die to self and give ourselves over to God for His purposes, we are setting ourselves apart. We are designating ourselves for a specific and divine use.

That is the purpose of this book…to assist you in dying to self and setting yourself apart that you might experience transformation, breakthrough and a new beginning in Him. This is consecration. Consecration properly and adequately cleanses and prepares you for the work ahead.

Many scientists debate the purpose of butterflies. They are pollinators; however, in comparison to bees, they are very poor ones. Because of the design of their bodies and the reach of their long proboscis (the straw-like portion of their mouths), butterflies are able to land on flowers and drink from their nectar without burying themselves within the bud. As a result, only small amounts of pollen cover their feet as they flit from blossom to blossom. Bees, on the other hand, become completely covered with pollen since their small bodies require they go deeper into the bloom. Hence, the reason they are our primary pollinators.

So what's the debate? Some scientists view butterflies as being helpful pollinators, despite the lesser amount of pollen they carry; while others feel they serve no purpose other than as a food source for predators and decoration for our environment.

I hold a different view. In addition to aiding the environment through pollination, I believe butterflies serve as a divine model of consecration and the faith one must have to both embark upon and successfully complete the process of Becoming. The transition from caterpillar to butterfly gives us the perfect picture of what it means to become a new creation in Christ Jesus. The transition from caterpillar to butterfly gives us the perfect picture of what it means to die in order to live.

Our journeys to being made new in Christ are not easy. And dying hurts. It was never meant to feel good. Sometimes the promise of our new lives seems so far away, but this divine visual aid helps us to have faith in what we do not yet see. The symbolism of a caterpillar's journey to butterfly gives us hope.

So how do we die? What does the dying process look like? There are a few steps to this process. But first, let's look at our friend the butterfly.

After a period of feasting on leaves, the caterpillar suddenly stops eating. It finds a safe place and enters into the protective casing we know as the chrysalis. The same must happen if we wish to consecrate ourselves for The LORD and His good works. We must stop eating and go into the secret place. That is, we must enter into a period of prayer and fasting where we will privately commune with The LORD. The chrysalis is our secret place. And in this secret place is where consecration will occur.

You may be wondering why consecration is necessary. The Word tells us that the gifts and calling of God come without repentance (Romans 11:29). Meaning, you can stray far from God's plan and ignore His call on your life and still operate in the gifts He has given you. God has placed special gifts in us all. It is our choice to use these gifts for the purpose of helping others and advancing His Kingdom here on earth. If we decide to reject Him and refuse to repent, these gifts still remain with us. He does not take them back.

However, if we acknowledge and answer His call on our lives with a resounding "Yes," then we are required to consecrate ourselves. We must be willing to give ourselves completely to the process of being washed clean. When we hear the call of God on our lives and understand who God has designed us to become, purity is critical in unlocking that design. By answering the call and consecrating ourselves, we prepare ourselves for the next stage…our commissioning. When we are commissioned by God, we are given divine authority to carry out specific plans on behalf of His Kingdom and for His Glory.

But before commissioning can even take place, we must get to the business of consecration. Again, once you have determined what and who God is calling you to become, consecration is essential. And this process is facilitated through prayer and fasting. By definition, consecration is a setting apart for specific use. It is the act of declaring or making something sacred. It is a process of cleansing and purification so we may be used as vessels for His Glory. Consequently, consecration requires a few things.

Consecration Requires Truth and Intimacy

Let's turn to The Word. John 13:5-8 illustrates the connection between consecration, truth and intimacy. Here, we see Jesus cleansing His disciples' feet before the Feast of the Passover.

"After that, He poured water into a basin and began to wash the disciples' feet, and to wipe them with the towel with which He was

girded. Then He came to Simon Peter. And Peter said to Him, 'Lord, are You washing my feet?' Jesus answered and said to him, 'What I am doing you do not understand now, but you will know after this.' Peter said to Him, 'You shall never wash my feet!' Jesus answered him, 'If I do not wash you, you have no part with Me.'"

~John 13:5-8, NKJV

Let's unpack this. In this exchange, Jesus was illustrating that we must be willing to serve one another by doing unto others as He has done for us. But this is also a clear teaching on the importance of being bathed and cleansed. Christ said that in order to have a part with and belong to Him, we must first be clean. If we have no part with Him, how can we be set apart? We can't. Being cleansed is being set apart and designated holy. This is the heart of consecration.

But let's look at this text a little more closely. Verse 5 expresses that Jesus was girded with a towel. He used that towel to wipe and cleanse their feet. Girded…meaning the towel was secured around His waist. Where else have we seen this concept of girding one's waist? Ephesians Chapter 6 (NKJV) gives us a detailed description of The Whole Armor of God. It instructs us to use this spiritual armor against the wiles of the devil. Each component of the armor serves a specific purpose. Verse 14a teaches us the significance of the Belt of Truth.

"Stand therefore, having girded your waist with truth…"

The towel girded around Jesus' waist represents far more than a simple cloth. This towel is representative of the truth, and we see it depicted as being wrapped around Jesus' core. From this, we clearly see that Jesus, who is also "the way, the **truth** and the life (John 14:6, NKJV)," is cleansing His disciples' feet with the Truth. He is cleansing them with the Word. He is cleansing them with Himself.

The truth makes us free (John 8:32). The truth changes and transforms us. The Truth makes us clean and whole. Walking and living in the truth of God, which is both His word as well as His Son Christ Jesus, rinses us of all impurities. Keeping ourselves bound and girded with the Truth of The Almighty Father, keeps us bathed in uprightness. When we are washed by the Word of God, we are consecrated and set apart.

But wait, there's more. In addition to illustrating the importance of being wiped clean and bathed in truth before we can belong to Jesus, the text at John Chapter 13 also proves that consecration requires intimacy. When the disciples asked Him where they should partake in their

Passover meal, Jesus gave them specific instructions that led them to a guest room in a man's home…a large upper room that would be prepared specifically for Jesus and the twelve. John 13:4 NKJV says that after their meal, Jesus "rose from supper and laid aside His garments, took a towel and girded Himself." This suggests that Christ removed His clothing and placed a towel securely around His waist. The towel He used to cover Himself was the same towel used to wipe their feet. This picture of the Truth wrapped in truth humbling himself before His disciples and cleansing their feet in a private place is a beautiful depiction of intimacy.

The LORD wants us to enter into the chrysalis with Him. He wants us to designate time to intimately commune with Him as He shares His truth with us. He wants to bathe and cleanse us in truth. He wants truth to secure us. He wants His truth to be at our core that we may find comfort and strength in it. He wants to shower us with Himself and make us spotless so we can have the honor of joining in on Kingdom assignments with Him. He wants us to *become* a new creature…a thing of beauty that will carry out His divine assignments with power and authority.

Consecration Requires Submission, Sacrifice and Surrender

Our flesh is corrupt and sinful. It does not wish to do the will of Jehovah God. If not subdued, our lives will be governed by it. Allowing our flesh to rule leads us down paths of unrighteousness, darkness and destruction.

"The mind governed by the flesh is hostile to God; it does not submit to God's law, nor can it do so."

~Romans 8:7

The text above says our flesh is hostile to God. Hostile! If you have ever dealt with someone who was hostile towards you, then you know that person was aggressive, combative, bitter and completely opposed to you, your thoughts, feelings or ideas. Many times, people reference the discomfort of having to endure hostile work or home environments. These surroundings are dysfunctional and anxiety inducing. They are oftentimes likened to warzones. Imagine that! Our flesh is like a warzone to the will of God. Our flesh is God's enemy. This is the God we love and serve, yet our flesh bucks against Him and aims to do the opposite of His will.

How do we subdue our flesh? How do we get it to line up with the will of God for our lives? The first way is by beating it into **submission**! Before you run away scared, let me explain. This is not a physical flogging. The way we submit to the Father is by denying our flesh. We starve it by rejecting sinful cravings that pull us out of alignment with The LORD. We say no to those immoral desires that satisfy our lustful hearts. We submit ourselves to God by saying "No" to temptation and every enticing seduction of the enemy. We submit ourselves to God by resisting the devil so he will flee from us (James 4:7).

When we submit to God, we willingly bow down to His authority and reign. We yield to His rule and power over our lives. We submit by accepting Christ Jesus as our Lord and King and by allowing His word to govern every aspect of our lives. As believers, our daily prayers and decrees should include the words spoken by the psalmist at Psalms 119:133, NKJV: "Direct my steps by Your word, and let no iniquity have dominion over me." Submitting to God means we mark ourselves as His territory. And sin should have no place or authority in God's domain.

After we have bowed down to the reign of God's precepts over our lives, the second way we subdue our flesh is by offering ourselves as a **sacrifice**. We should be willing to climb upon the altar and die, giving ourselves over completely to God's plans and desires for our lives. When we give ourselves as a sacrificial offering to God, we are saying that it is no longer us who lives, but Christ who dwells in us. Sacrificing ourselves means we are ready to be tested and tried by the fire. When we lay upon the altar and allow the flames of adversity to consume us, our moral character is strengthened. When we offer our lives sacrificially, our outward man burns away and releases a fragrance pleasing to The Father.

"And burn the whole ram on the altar. It is a burnt offering to the Lord. It is a pleasing aroma, a food offering to the Lord."

~Exodus 29:18, ESV

"And walk in love, as Christ loved us and gave himself up for us, a fragrant offering and sacrifice to God."

~Ephesians 5:2, ESV

Sacrificially giving ourselves over to the will of The Father shows deep respect and appreciation for the ransom Jesus willingly paid for us on the cross. He lovingly and willfully agree to be tortured and crucified so that we could receive salvation and have a place with Him in God's

Kingdom. When we show Him the same love in return, we allow Him to come alive in us.

"I have been crucified with Christ; it is no longer I who live, but Christ lives in me; and the life which I now live in the flesh I live by faith in the Son of God, who loved me and gave Himself for me."

~Galatians 2:20, NKJV

God wants to abide in us just as much as He wants us to abide in Him. Our communing with God is not limited to the four walls of the church. Our relationship with Him extends beyond that. When we are in relationship with The Father, it is ongoing and knows no limits. He wants to be with us. When our lives are fully intertwined with Him and with His word, we carry His presence with us at all times.

At Exodus 25:8, the LORD spoke to Moses and instructed him to have His people construct a sanctuary that He may dwell among them. The presence of The LORD appeared as a cloud resting above the tabernacle. When the cloud of The Lord moved, His people would disassemble the tabernacle and follow. When the cloud stopped, God's people knew to reassemble the sanctuary and set up camp in that place (Numbers 9:15-23).

God wants this same relationship with us today. But it is vital that we recognize that we are God's tabernacles. We are His houses of prayer…His sanctuaries. And wherever He leads, we should follow. We should sacrifice our all in exchange for His presence. Wherever the Spirit of God goes, we should go. Whatever He is doing, we should seek to be a part of it. When we give ourselves to becoming His houses of prayer, we are led by and carry His Glory.

In scripture, the tabernacle had an altar. This altar was lit by The LORD Himself, and His people were instructed to never allow the flame to burn out. This command holds true for us today. Once God lights His fire in us, we should never allow it to go out. We should fall so deeply in love with Our Father that our spiritual altars burn with an eternal flame so intense that we remain in a perpetual state of sacrifice. We should sacrifice ourselves willingly, lovingly and continuously to The Father by giving Him our lives daily.

"You yourselves like living stones are being built up as a spiritual house, to be a holy priesthood, to offer spiritual sacrifices acceptable to God through Jesus Christ."

~1 Peter 2:5, ESV

The Creator of all that is seen and unseen cares so deeply about each one of us that He is building us up to be sanctuaries. As we come to The Father, He sees us as He sees His Son. We are likened unto Christ. We are like living stones! As we are made into houses of worship, we become holy priests and, thus, offer spiritual sacrifices to God through the blood of Jesus.

Once we have submitted to the Highest Authority and have offered ourselves as living sacrifices to Him, the third step in subduing the flesh is **surrender**. When we surrender to God, we are waving the white flag of capitulation. We are relinquishing complete control and agreeing to no longer resist the will of The Father. In surrender, we release all hostility, anxiety and fear and give everything — good and bad — over to God.

But surrender is not one-sided. It's an agreement. During times of war, one side may agree to surrender to the other in exchange for something in return. When two parties enter into an agreed upon arrangement, hostility is neutralized; a compromise is met and a covenant is formed. Jehovah wants this with His people. He wants this with you and me. He wants the hostility of our flesh to be neutralized so we can form a treaty with Him.

But this is not just any treaty. Most treaties or agreements represent an equal, or somewhat equal, exchange. Not with God. When we enter into covenant with Him through the act of surrender, we come out on top! We are the ones who get the most out of the deal. He wants to give us "beauty for ashes, the oil of joy for mourning, the garment of praise for the spirit of heaviness… (Isaiah 61:3, NKJV)." We are instructed to cast all our cares on Him (1 Peter 5:7). He wants us to lay every worry, fear and concern at His feet and say, *"Take it, Father. I surrender all my burdens to You knowing You will give me peace, joy and victory in exchange."*

Isn't that amazing? Our Father knows there is nothing we could ever give Him that would be equal to what He offers us, yet He continues to offer us good things anyway. He is so loving, gracious and kind that He will take our brokenness and give us riches in return. As long as our lives are postured in surrender, He will give us our hearts' desires.

But God doesn't just want our problems and afflictions. He wants everything about us. He wants us to surrender all unto Him. He wants our gifts, talents, triumphs and victories. He wants us to hand it all to Him, trusting that

He will give us even better in return. It is His desire to perfect everything concerning us, to give us life more abundantly and cause our cups to overflow.

Why does He do this? Why does He want us to surrender everything, both good and bad, knowing it pales in comparison to what He offers in return? He wants our surrender so He can be glorified. God wants us to glorify, praise, honor and worship Him.

Isaiah 61:3 continues on to say, "…that they may be called trees of righteousness, the planting of the LORD, that He may be glorified." Jehovah wants to give us beauty for ashes so that he can plant us in righteousness so that we, in turn, will exalt and glorify Him. Surrender is an act of worship. Handing over all our worldly cares in exchange for the opportunity to adore and love on God is the most beautiful expression of affection in His eyes. It tells God that He is above all things in our lives and that He is our number one priority.

When we carry an abundance of burdens and worry; when we shoulder responsibilities and commitments—even those that arise due to blessings in our lives—we are essentially telling God that we don't need Him…that we are bigger than He is. But we do need Him. And we are not bigger than He is…not even close.

Living a sacrificial life, fully submitted and surrendered to God is a vital part of consecration. When we live a life of complete submission, sacrifice and surrender to Our Heavenly Father, we are telling Him that we are willing to be used as His vessels. God wants to work in us and through us that we might carry His Glory and impact the lives of others. This can only happen when we submit to His authority, sacrifice ourselves on the altar and fully surrender our all to Him. This submission, sacrifice and surrender must be done daily. But it is also achieved on deeper levels through the process of prayer and fasting.

Consecration Requires Obedience and Faith

In order for consecration to be achieved through prayer and fasting, we must be able to walk in obedience and faith. However, to be able to demonstrate these concepts in our lives, we must have an accurate picture of what they are and how they function together.

According to the Oxford English Dictionary, obedience is defined as "compliance with an order, request, or law or submission to another's authority." It is a state of being dutiful, respectful and conforming to a perceived power. It is a humble agreement and observance to a set of established precepts. Obedience is recognizing God as the Highest Authority and, subsequently, hearkening and yielding to His directives and commands.

The same source describes faith as "complete trust or confidence in someone or something." From a spiritual standpoint, it is a "strong belief in God or in the doctrines of a religion, based on spiritual apprehension rather than proof." Faith is a deep belief and hope beyond what is seen with our natural eyes (Hebrews 11:1). It is an unwavering conviction rooted in the promises of God.

So, how do obedience and faith work together? Obedience and faith have such an interwoven relationship that it's hard to tell where one begins and the other ends. It's an unbroken exchange—a constant cause and effect—that makes it almost impossible to tell which came first. When we have strong faith in God, then we are obedient to His Word and will for our lives. In return, He is faithful and just to fulfill the promises that He has made to us. Consequently, seeing the manifestation of fulfilled promises builds our faith, which, in turn, strengthens our commitment to continued obedience. It's a beautiful divine cycle that produces countless Kingdom rewards.

Awaiting the manifestation of the promises of God in our lives hinges upon the divine relationship between these two concepts. Take Anna the prophetess for example. She remained at the temple, day and night, and, both, obediently and faithfully served God through a life committed to prayer and fasting. What was she awaiting? She was awaiting the arrival of the promised Messiah, Jesus Christ (Luke 2:36-38).

Like Anna, Simeon was also awaiting the coming of the Savior and the promise that he would indeed see the Christ before he departed this earth. God's word describes Simeon as being a man who was "just and devout." The Holy Spirit was upon him, and he lived a life of faithfulness and obedience to The LORD (Luke 2:25-26).

In this same biblical account, Jesus' earthly parents also show us a worthy example of the obedience and faith required for consecration and fulfilled promises. According to the Law of Moses, three things were to happen: Jesus was to be circumcised at 8 days after birth (Luke 2:21); Mary was to fulfill a required purification period by avoiding contact with anything sacred and staying out of the sanctuary for 33 days after giving birth (Leviticus 12); and upon completion of the 33 days, Mary and Joseph were to take Jesus to the temple and present Him to the LORD as well as present an offering of two turtledoves (Luke 2:22-24).

All involved in this account received a manifested promise because of their obedience and faith. Anna fasted and prayed and remained at the temple for decades. This unwavering dedication resulted in her seeing the promised Messiah. Simeon blessed God, held the infant and prophesied that Jesus was God's salvation, light and glory (Luke 2:29-32). He glorified The Father for keeping His word and allowing him the privilege and honor of seeing the coming of the Savior before he died.

Mary and Joseph saw the fulfillment of a promise, as well. When the Angel of The LORD appeared to Mary and told her that she would give birth to a son, he promised this child would be great and he would be called the Son of God (Luke 1:32). We see the fulfillment of that greatness in response to their obedience at Luke 2:39-40:

"When Jesus' parents had fulfilled all the requirements of the law of the Lord, they returned home to Nazareth in Galilee. There the child grew up healthy and strong. He was filled with wisdom, and God's favor was on him."

Here we see a direct relationship between the obedience of Mary and Joseph and the fulfilled promise of God. They were obedient to the law and saw the manifestation of God's word, which undoubtedly strengthened their faith going forward.

As we move in deeper levels of obedience, we rise to higher levels of faith. And as we go from faith to faith, we affirm our allegiance and loyalty to the Father by obediently listening to and heeding His every command. Obediently listening to The Father is vital for our salvation. Hardening our hearts and refusing to follow the commands of God results in a severed relationship with Him (Zechariah 7:11-14). But when we "diligently obey the voice of The LORD (Zechariah 6:15; Deuteronomy 28:1)," His promises to us are fulfilled. Those fulfilled promises foster trust. It takes trust to believe in those things that we do not yet see. It takes trust to hold firmly to that which we hope. It takes trust to wait patiently on the manifestations of His promises. And trusting in Him is the heart of faith.

But we can't explore faith and obedience without mentioning Abraham. Abraham's story shows us that obedience is also a test of faith. When Abram was 99 years of age, God appeared to him and called him to lead an obedient and faithful life. God changed his name to Abraham and promised him the reward of "countless descendants" in exchange for his obedience to the terms of their covenant. The covenantal agreement was that every male descendant of Abraham be circumcised. God then told Abraham that He was changing the name of his wife from Sarai to Sarah and that she, at age 90, would give birth to a son who should be named Isaac (Genesis 17).

Some years later, God again called out to Abraham, instructing him to take Isaac to one of the mountains in the land of Moriah and sacrifice him as a burnt offering to The LORD. Abraham did not hesitate to show his obedience to God's request. The next morning, he packed up Isaac, two servants and some supplies and traveled to the place that Jehovah had instructed. Once the proper location was found, he bound his son, whom he loved dearly, laid him on top of the altar and raised the knife to kill him. At that very moment, the Angel of The LORD called out to Abraham saying, "Don't lay a hand on the boy!...Do not hurt him in any way, for now I know that you truly fear God. You have not withheld from me even your son, your only son (Genesis 22:12)."

Not only did Jehovah stop Abraham from sacrificing his son, but also He provided a suitable offering—a ram in the bush. Abraham sacrificed the ram as a burnt offering to The LORD and named the place "Jehovah-Jireh" which means "The LORD will provide (Genesis 22:13-14)." We see here that the testing of Abraham's faith and obedience strengthened his faith in seeing God as a provider. When we are obedient, God is faithful, and, as a result, our faith level is taken to new heights. God takes us from faith to faith. This means a measure of faith is required to move to deeper and higher levels of faith (Romans 1:17).

Abraham's faith was tested. And because of his obedience, God blessed Abraham and his descendants.

"I will certainly bless you. I will multiply your descendants beyond number, like the stars in the sky and the sand on the seashore. Your descendants will conquer the cities of their enemies. And through your descendants all the nations of the earth will be blessed—all because you have obeyed me."

~Genesis 22:17-18

Prayer for the Requirements of Consecration

Heavenly Father, it is my desire to enter into a time of consecration with You. Place in me all that is required to be wholly cleansed and set apart for Your divine use. Remove all hindrances and inhibitions. I vow to enter into a time of intimacy with You. Wrap me in truth. I promise to keep Your truth at my core. Help me to completely submit, sacrifice and surrender myself to You and Your perfect will. I declare that I have the faith it takes to be obedient. Where I am lacking in faith, help my unbelief. You are my God and I trust You. Have Your way. In the Mighty Name of Jesus, Amen.

Declarations for the Requirements of Consecration

I declare I possess the requirements of consecration.

I declare I am rooted in truth.

I declare I have let go of all distractions and hindrances that might prevent me from entering into a place of intimacy with God.

I declare I am fully submitted, sacrificed and surrendered to The LORD.

I declare I am fully obedient to the commands of God, and my faith in Him and in His ways is stronger than ever.

CONSECRATION IN THE CHRYSALIS

"He who is completely sanctified, or cleansed from all sin, and dies in this state, is fit for glory."
- Adam Clarke

Before the advent of a butterfly, a specific sequence of events must transpire. The caterpillar must die in order to live as the creation it was designed to become. This dying in order to become is a process. It is a process of dying to the old and being rebirthed in the new. It is a time of complex details geared towards transformation, breakthrough and new beginnings. This process is one of repurposing, redefining and restructuring. It is a complete cleansing of all impurities that would inhibit one from being used as a new vessel. This process prepares us to be used in a new capacity that we may reach new heights. This process is consecration, and consecration occurs in the chrysalis — the chrysalis is the secret place of consecration.

Right now, you are that caterpillar. And just like the caterpillar, you must embrace the requirements of consecration in order for a life-changing transformation to take place.

In the previous section, we highlighted the requirements for consecration. Those requirements are: **truth and intimacy; submission, sacrifice and surrender; and obedience and faith**. Metaphorically speaking, we can see that the caterpillar is held to this same set of prerequisites. Let's examine them.

Truth and Intimacy. A caterpillar has no idea why it is prompted to stop eating, find a secret place on a leaf and allow it's outer covering to be shed, revealing its chrysalis. It accepts this intimate process as truth. A truth that must take place. It doesn't resist. It doesn't keep secrets or hide old hurts and wounds. It enters in—fully abandoned and exposed—and waits to be changed in the intimate place by truth…the truth of what it is meant to become.

Submission, Sacrifice and Surrender. When a caterpillar instinctively enters into the chrysalis experience, it is willfully submitting to a power greater than its own. It is saying, "Have your way. I submit to your authority." Once it has submitted by entering the chrysalis, it offers itself as a sacrifice and surrenders all. The caterpillar is literally melted down into a slurry…a biological soup. It no longer resembles what it once was. It relinquishes all control and places its trust in a future that is unknown.

Obedience and Faith. It takes obedience for the caterpillar to even enter the chrysalis. And it takes faith to know that the slush to which it has been reduced will eventually come together to create the beautiful being it was always destined to become.

The caterpillar is our example of being fully surrendered and obedient to The Father. Think about it. All we need is the heart and commitment of a tiny, furry worm to receive our promise of transformation, breakthrough and new beginnings. If faith the size of a mustard seed can move mountains, then caterpillar-sized commitment and obedience can surely lead to breakthrough (Matthew 17:20).

The caterpillar dies so that it can live. This is what we do through the act of consecration. We die to self so that we can be saved and reborn as a new creation. Consecration is lifesaving. This obedient act can literally save your soul. Let's look at the word "save." Many people see the word "save" and automatically think of it as meaning "to rescue or keep safe." But "save" also means to preserve; to keep and store up for future use; to put aside or set aside for specific use. This is exactly what consecration accomplishes. Consecration purifies, refines and sets the believer aside for a special purpose.

James 1:21 NKJV says, "Therefore lay aside all filthiness and overflow of wickedness, and receive with meekness the implanted word, which is able to save your souls." God wants to embed His word on the inside of us. Christ Jesus wants to be implanted in us. This implantation can only take place when we humble ourselves and separate from every unclean thing. When we enter into the secret place with meek hearts and allow the process of consecration to take place, our lives are saved and set aside for specific use.

As we are saved through consecration, three things happen: transformation, breakthrough and a new beginning. In biblical times, when a person was consecrated, they were anointed with oil as a part of the act. I believe that as you sit with Holy Spirit in the secret place, God's Glory will anoint you with the oils of transformation, breakthrough and new beginnings. I believe that when you humbly and willfully enter the chrysalis, God will pour out His Transforming Anointing, His Breaker Anointing and His Renewing Anointing.

As the caterpillar is being transformed into the butterfly, its wings begin to develop small mirror-like scales that will be responsible for absorbing and reflecting light.

This happens to us in the chrysalis, as well. I believe the Transforming oil of The Father causes our hearts and minds to be so pure and undefiled that when we look in the mirror, we see the perfect reflection of God. The Transforming oil brings about such a miraculous metamorphosis, that when others look at us, they see Christ replicated. In Genesis 1:26 NKJV, God said, "Let Us make man in Our image, according to Our likeness…" God went on to form man from the dust. Man was formed from sand. That was no mistake. Do you know what else is made from sand? Mirrors! When God made man, He wanted to look at His creation and see the reflection of Himself. He wanted to see His likeness. Through consecration, the Transforming oil of The Father changes us into a mirror image of Him. It should be our hearts desire to resemble our Heavenly Father. When we emerge from our time of consecration, our wings should act as mirrors capable of absorbing God's light as well as reflecting His image back up to Him.

Once we are transformed, it is God's will to see us carry out the plans He has for our lives. He wants us to go forth courageously and touch the lives of others. This can't happen if we remain in the chrysalis. The LORD wants us to take the wisdom, knowledge, understanding, boldness and new purpose that was developed in the secret place with

Him and share it with others that they, too, can be encouraged to enter into their own time of consecration. In order to do this, we have to break out. We need to break through the barriers and ceilings that once prevented us from moving forward. We need to break out of destructive cycles and limiting patterns and beliefs. Once transformation takes place, we are ready for the Breaker anointing. Jehovah is the One who breaks. He is the Breaker. Once real change has been established in us, I believe God will pour out the oil of Breakthrough. Like the butterfly, we will breakthrough…we will emerge, and He will be with us.

"The one who breaks open will come up before them; They will break out, Pass through the gate, and go out by it; Their king will pass before them, with the LORD at their head."
Micah 2:13, NKJV

After transformation and breakthrough, the creature is ready to start its New Beginning as a butterfly. This truth applies to us, as well. When the oil of New Beginning is poured out, we are made new.

"Therefore, if anyone is in Christ, he is a new creation; old things have passed away; behold all things have become new."
2 Corinthians 5:17, NKJV

I believe as God releases His Renewing anointing, we are made ready to spread our wings and fly to new heights. Isaiah 40:31 NKJV says, "But those who wait on the LORD shall renew their strength; They shall mount up with wings like eagles, they shall run and not be weary, They shall walk and not faint." Though they seem delicate, a butterfly's wings are strong and powerful. They are capable of flying long distances and amazing heights. The LORD wants this for us. He wants us to experience the transformation that brings about renewal. He wants to renew a steadfast spirit within us (Psalm 51:10). He wants to see us soar, walk and run for the advancement of His Kingdom and never grow weary. He wants to anoint us with fresh oil—a renewing oil—that will cause us to flourish and bear good fruit (Psalm 92:10-15).

Consecration and the Number 8

We know that Consecration is the action of cleansing, declaring and making something or oneself sacred and set apart for specific use. But what does this have to do with the number eight? Why is this particular period of prayer and fasting an eight day journey?

The number 8 symbolizes new beginnings. The entire purpose of being transformed in the chrysalis and receiving breakthrough is so that we can each move forward in our new beginnings. There are many instances of the number eight in scripture that mark significant times of new beginnings. Here are a few:

- In the beginning, the earth was void and without form. Darkness was all around. In exactly 8 steps, God initiated a new beginning. He formed all of creation in 8 stages (See Genesis 1:3; 1:6; 1:9; 1:11; 1:14; 1:20; 1:24 and 1:26).
- In Genesis chapter 8, we see Noah, his wife, his 3 sons and their wives emerge from the ark after The Great Flood. Noah and his family were the only human survivors, and their total was eight. This was a new beginning for creation.
- In Genesis 17:9-13 and Leviticus 12:3, we see The LORD requiring that every male child be circumcised on the 8th day of birth. This was a covenant between God and His people. It was symbolic of complete submission to God and the commencement of a new beginning with Him. Although we are not required to undergo physical circumcision any longer, as His children, our hearts should be spiritually circumcised and fully submitted to Him.

All The Father needs is 8 days alone with us in the secret place of the chrysalis in order to reshape, repurpose and transform us. After your 8 days of dedicated prayer and fasting, you will be ready to experience breakthrough and a new beginning. You will be a new creation, marked pure and holy...fit for glory!

Prayer for Consecration in the Chrysalis:

Heavenly Father, I humble myself before You as I embark upon this 8 day journey of being purified, marked holy and set apart for Your glory and purposes. It is my desire to be made new... to break free of all that has been trying to place a lid on me and to launch out into my new beginning. In order to do this Father, I need Your oil. I need Your anointing that comes by Your Spirit. I cannot do this by my might nor by my power, but by Your Spirit, God. It is the anointing that transforms. It is the anointing that breaks yokes. It is the anointing that makes all things new. Create in me a clean heart, Heavenly Father, that I may be deemed ready and worthy of your anointing.

In the mighty name of Jesus, Amen.

Declarations for Consecration in the Chrysalis:

I declare that, like the caterpillar, I have the heart, courage and obedience necessary to enter into my chrysalis experience.

I declare that I will lay aside all filth and uncleanliness so my soul will be saved and set aside for divine use.

I declare I am entering the chrysalis with a bowed head and a humble heart.

I declare God's Transforming, Breaker and Renewing anointing over my life.

I declare a Number 8, New Beginning blessing over my life.

I declare I will be transformed.

I declare I will breakthrough.

I declare every lid, ceiling, chain, box and restriction will be broken off of my life.

I declare I will emerge as a new creation in Christ Jesus.

I declare I will emerge as a mirror image of The Father.

I declare my newly formed wings will reflect His majesty.

I declare I will be consecrated, sanctified and fit for glory.

I declare these truths in the name of Jesus!

EXHORTATION

"Just when the caterpillar thought the world was over, it became a butterfly."

The above is a popular quote by Chinese philosopher Zhuangzi. And though I do not subscribe to ancient eastern philosophies or practices, this particular quote does give one cause to ponder and question. Do caterpillars think? Are they cognizant of the call to the chrysalis? Do they see it as a call to their unfortunate end? Or does the caterpillar know it is destined to become a butterfly but just does not know what the steps are to that new life?

Whatever the answers to these questions are, this imagery gives us a remarkable illustration of dying to self…sacrificing the flesh and surrendering all to become a new creation in Christ Jesus. As stated previously, this dying to self is consecration. It is committing yourself to a renewal of purpose. Just as the caterpillar is beckoned to the chrysalis, we also, as believers, are beseeched and exhorted to a time of metamorphosis and change (2 Corinthians 5:17)…to a time of consecration.

This book's foundational scripture, found at Romans 12:1-2, serves as an exhortation to the entire body of Christ. According to Dictionary.com, an exhortation is "the act or process of exhorting; an utterance, discourse, or address conveying urgent advice or recommendations." We are invited, persuaded, and encouraged to present our entire beings as sacrifices for the purposes of being renewed and transformed. As followers of Christ Jesus, God desires to use us. He invites us to partner with Him in work for His Kingdom. But partnering with The Most High requires being processed and elevated into new levels. It is because of this that we will receive an exhortation to a time of consecration.

Just before the caterpillar enters the chrysalis, it receives biological promptings and triggers. The same is true for us in a sense. Before every significant time of spiritual growth and change, there will be an invitation from God to set yourself apart…to designate your life and gifting for His good use and purposes.

Exhortation in a Dream

"For God speaks again and again, though people do not recognize it. He speaks in dreams, in visions of the night, when deep sleep falls on people as they lie in their beds. He whispers in their ears and terrifies them with warnings. He makes them turn from doing wrong; he keeps them from pride. He protects them from the grave, from crossing over the river of death." ~Job 33:14-18 NLT

God speaks to us in our dreams. When our minds are quiet and still and our bodies are at rest, He speaks. When outside distractions of family, work, children, bills, cell phones, technology, social media and politics no longer have our full attentions, God visits us. The noise of everyday life can easily drown out God's voice. Thankfully, He is gracious and loving enough to bring us messages in the night. He whispers warnings in our ears and seals instructions on our hearts. It is up to us to heed His wise council and carry out His plans.

At this point you may be wondering why I'm sharing all of this with you. I'm doing so because the invitation to write this book began with a dream.

One night, I dreamt I was watching a little squirrel…at least that is what I called it in my dream. It was a bizarre looking animal with two tails. This little squirrel was in the center of the room performing ballet during a recital. She was dancing quite beautifully. She was captivating. Everyone was in awe.

A famous comedian standing next to me decided to use my cell phone to call the woman who had adopted this little squirrel as her own. He was making jokes, as comedians do…unfortunately, they were inappropriate and offensive. In a failed attempt to compliment her on her "daughter's" performance, he angered and insulted the mother. She was furious.

When he got off the phone, I snatched it away and said to him, "Now she has my number and will think I had something to do with this."

After the recital, there was a buffet-style reception. Again, I found myself standing next to yet another well-known comedian, different from the one before. We were standing near the food tables.

Suddenly, the mother of the dancing squirrel emerged from a backroom where all the mothers of the dancers were. She was dressed in a black, form-fitting dress. Her complexion was a sickly pallor. She had black serpents for hair that seemed to creep up the wall in a slow, symbiotic-type motion as she stood against it.

The comedian I was standing with began talking about the woman. Like the first comedian, his comments were jokes...loud, inappropriate and offensive. In an attempt to dissuade him from engaging with what was clearly demonic, I hushed him. He ignored my urgings to silence his behavior. His wisecracks continued despite her glare of disapproval.

She then began walking though the room, causing something mysterious to happen to all the others who were in attendance. They all began to vanish. The comic began laughing and clownishly spewing nonsense like, "She can't do that to me! I go to church! That happened to them because they don't go to church!"

The distance between me and her was quickly fading as she glided closer and closer. I lunged toward her and shouted, "In the name of Jesus, I rebuke you! In the mighty name of Jesus!" I was bold and spoke with confidence and authority. But nothing happened. In fact, the situation seemed to worsen. The people who had vanished suddenly reappeared. They were surrounding and grabbing at me. Suddenly, it seemed as though she was gone and only the people remained—possessed, manipulated and controlled, left with orders to carry out her evil plots and schemes against me…like zombies incapable of thinking for themselves.

I kept shouting, "In Jesus' name! In Jesus' name!" But all I could see were hands coming at me, reaching for me. And then, I woke up.

I was rattled by this dream. Upon awakening, I immediately thought, "Why didn't it work?" I had spoken with authority and commanded this evil to be gone in the name of Jesus, yet, unrelentingly, it kept coming. The evil kept pressing forward to pursue me. So I asked God, "Father, why did it not work?" The answer was immediately revealed through Matthew 17:14-21.

And when they had come to the multitude, a man came to Him, kneeling down to Him and saying, "Lord, have mercy on my son, for he is an epileptic and suffers severely; for he often falls into the fire and often into the water. So I brought him to Your disciples, but they could not cure him." Then Jesus answered and said, "O faithless and perverse generation, how long shall I be with you? How long shall I bear with you? Bring him here to Me." And Jesus rebuked the demon, and it came out of him; and the child was cured from that very hour. Then the disciples came to Jesus privately and said, "Why could we not cast it out?" So Jesus said to them, "Because of your unbelief; for assuredly, I say to you, if you have faith as a mustard seed, you will say to this mountain, 'Move from here to there,' and it will move; and nothing will be impossible for you. However, this kind does not go out except by prayer and fasting." ~Matthew 17:14-21 NKJV

In this biblical account, Jesus' disciples could not understand why they were unable to cast the demon out of the boy. Jesus told them it was because of their lack of faith, calling them a "faithless generation." He also added that this particular type of demon that was plaguing the boy could only be driven out by prayer and fasting.

As soon as I read this scripture, I knew immediately that this dream was a divine exhortation…a call from God to enter into a period of prayer and fasting. If I wanted to move further and deeper in the things of God, I needed to consecrate myself. If I expected to walk in my full authority in Christ, then I must offer myself as a living sacrifice. I recently heard God speak the phrase "the meaner, the cleaner." What He was saying was the meaner the demon you encounter, the cleaner your heart must be. And not only must your heart be clean, your faith level must be strong.

After realizing I was being invited to a time of prayer and fasting, I took another look at the aforementioned bible text. I slowly pulled this scripture apart. There is something important here to note—something I had never considered or been taught. Let's pretend for a moment that the disciples knew that that particular type of demon could only be cast out through prayer and fasting. Would they have decided there on the spot to enter into a period of fasting and praying before helping the man? Would they have told the man to bring his son back in a day? 3 days? 21 days? Or even 40 days? No. Of course not. To tell the man they needed to spend time fasting and praying before they could be of any assistance would have been absurd. Considering the seriousness of the boy's state, it would have proven deadly…dangerous, at best.

So, that lends the question…what was Jesus really saying to the disciples? How could they have been prepared and ready to aid in deliverance that first required prayer and fasting? The answer is quite simple. In order to be ready to combat that specific type of demonic attack, the disciples would have needed to live a lifestyle of prayer and fasting. They would have had to commit to prayer and fasting as a normal, routine part of their ministry. Had they maintained a consistent practice of prayer and fasting, then they would have been able to cast out that demon. Had they earnestly devoted regular intervals of time to prayer and fasting, they would have had the faith level and clean hearts required. They would have been well-oiled, properly equipped, demon-slaying machines.

There is another important revelation here. And that is that Jesus, himself, clearly lived a lifestyle of prayer and fasting. This text, in combination with many others, supports this conclusion. Jesus' life on earth was the ultimate example of how we should live. He set certain standards of Kingdom living and instructed others to follow. And that command to, "Follow Me," did not just mean in the geographical sense, but in every way.

"Then Jesus said to His disciples, 'If anyone desires to come after Me, let him deny himself, and take up his cross, and follow Me. For whoever desires to save his life will lose it, but whoever loses his life for My sake will find it. For what profit is it to a man if he gains the whole world, and loses his own soul? Or what will a man give in exchange for his soul?'"

~Matthew 16:24-26 NKJV

Jesus wanted His disciples, His followers and His church today to "follow" His every example. And one of those examples is prayer and fasting as a regular part of one's lifestyle. Jesus is neither doubleminded nor hypocritical. Therefore, He would not have expected His disciples to routinely pray and fast if He, himself, was not already doing so. Jesus leads by example and did not subject His disciples (nor does He subject us) to any expectations that He was not meeting also.

We can't follow Christ Jesus if we are distracted. In my dream, the squirrel was just that…a distraction. It captured everyone's attention. The enemy doesn't just distract us with things that are troublesome and problematic. He will also attempt to distract with things that seem impressive, as was the case with the beautiful, dancing squirrel. If he can get your attention away from that which is important, he can attack. This is another reason why it is important to spend time in prayer and fasting. Tuning out the world and all its noise and chaos puts you in a position to focus and tune in to the voice of God. The more we focus on Him, the more discernment we will develop and the less inclined we will be to waste precious time, attention and resources on things that are not of God.

Another important element of the exhortation I received in the dream was the "jokers," those "comedians" who spoke without weighing the consequences of their words. This dream issued a warning to be cautious of those who are not good stewards over their words and who do not use them wisely. Surrounding yourself with people such as this can cause you to become caught in the middle of a spiritual battle that is not meant for you. As in this dream, I took on spiritual warfare that was not my assignment—an assignment for which I was not prepared. When we spend time fasting and praying, we become certain of our assignments. We develop intimacy with The Father and He makes His instructions clear to us. We learn who and what to allow around us. Once you make prayer and fasting a normal part of your lifestyle, you learn how to properly guard your ear and eye gates and you know what company to keep. When you fast and pray regularly, you surrender your entire self as a vessel for God's Kingdom use. Protecting the purity of that vessel is of utmost importance.

In my dream, the demonic woman had serpents coming from her head. She placed a manipulative spell over all the other people causing them to come after me. She was likely representative of a python spirit. The spirit of python is the spirit of divination which is witchcraft. In Acts 16:16-18, Paul and Silas encounter a slave girl who practiced witchcraft, specifically fortune-telling for her masters' gain. She was possessed with the spirit of divination. Some translations refer to it as the spirit of python. This spirit constricts and seeks to crush and squeeze the life out. But Jesus came that we might have life and life more abundantly (John 10:10).

As a result of this dream, I was led to enter into an 8 day fast—8 being the spiritual number for new beginnings. Initially, I thought I might solicit the participation of others and fast corporately. But then Holy Spirit gave me the following: *Consecration in the Chrysalis: 8 Days of Prayer and Fasting for Transformation, Breakthrough and New Beginnings.* I thought to myself, "Wow…that's a book title!"

And so here we are — me, having been obedient to write it…and you, being obedient to read and follow it.

PREPARATION

"By failing to prepare, you are preparing to fail."
~Benjamin Franklin

Before the caterpillar enters its chrysalis, it spends time gorging on nourishment. The caterpillar instinctively moves from eating normal quantities to consuming leaves in massive amounts. Before embarking on its life-changing journey, it spends time in preparation. If it did not, it would not have the nourishment required to successfully transition from caterpillar to butterfly. Housed in a protective covering with no nutrients and no way out—with processes only semi-complete—it would surely die if it did not adequately feed itself before the process began.

Just as the caterpillar ensures it has all the proper nutrients necessary to sustain its life during its next phase, we, also, should spend time preparing before entering a time of consecration.

Whether it be in the spirit or in the natural, the process of preparation is important for the success of any lasting change. Before building a home, the construction team reviews blueprints and floorplans and arranges for the delivery of all essential tools, hardware, lumber and personnel necessary to execute the plan.

> "For which of you, desiring to build a tower, does not first sit down and count the cost, whether he has enough to complete it?"
>
> ~Luke 14:28, ESV

Before the birth of a baby, parents make preparations for its arrival, ensuring everything needed for the comfort and care of their newborn is in place. It is wise to make preparations beforehand so that everything needed to successfully build, create, sustain, receive or process something is in position and ready to play its part.

This time of prayer and fasting calls for at least 3 days of preparation before beginning the 8 core days of the fast. This 3-day period is groundwork. It is a time of laying a strong foundation that will provide lasting support for permanent change. This period of preparation should be governed by prayer and marked by 3 significant actions:

Seek, Worship, EAT.

- **Seek:**
  Although, this entire fast is for the express purpose of transformation, breakthrough and new beginnings, it is important to know which areas or situations in

your life require this transformation, breakthrough and new beginning. What elements of your spiritual character need bolstering? What are you *seeking*? Is it peace, unity or insight? Perhaps it's wisdom, knowledge and understanding. Maybe purity in heart or direction for your next steps. Whatever it is, spend time in prayer earnestly seeking purpose. Get specific with God. Ask questions and set goals. Let your requests be made known to Him. Your specific purpose for this fast will be revealed through prayer.

"Ask, and it will be given to you; seek, and you will find; knock, and it will be opened to you. For everyone who asks receives, and he who seeks finds, and to him who knocks it will be opened."
~Matthew 7:7-8, NKJV

- **Worship:**
  This 3 day, pre-fast period should also be a time of pure worship to The Father. This should be easy for a mature believer because our hearts should be in a perpetual position of worship to The LORD. Worship is a lifestyle and it is imperative that we keep ourselves clothed in a garment of worship.

So, what is worship? Worship is posturing our hearts to shower our Heavenly Father with love, respect and adoration. It is an intimate connection that should exist solely between us and The LORD. Worship is honoring, revering, glorifying, exalting, elevating, extoling and praising Him. Worship belongs only to God…not to anyone or anything else. When we worship The Father with our whole hearts, minds and bodies, we acknowledge His awesomeness; we humble ourselves under His Power and Might; we recognize that He is the very air we breathe. We laud Him because He is above all things. His eyes roam about the earth, seeking those who will worship Him in spirit and in truth. He is searching for hearts who are committed to serving Him and Him alone (John 4:23-24; Matthew 4:10).

- **EAT:**
During this time of preparation, it is imperative that we be full of the Word. Just as the caterpillar begins to gorge on nutrients before entering the chrysalis, we must also get fat on the word of God. When we feast on the Word, we store it up in our spirits that it may be quickened at the proper time. When the word is

quickened, it is activated and able to revive that which God has placed within us. This fast will not be easy. We will experience physical, emotional, mental and spiritual discomforts. It doesn't feel good to be melted down into slush and reassembled. We will need the word to sustain and nourish us during those uncomfortable times.

Also consider this…during this consecration, you will be required to climb upon the altar and offer yourself as a living sacrifice. In scripture, the sacrifice was a fatted animal. These animals were set aside specifically for sacrifice to The LORD. The fat of the animal was considered the choicest cut, and this fat belonged to God. We should present ourselves to God in a way that is pleasing to Him. So it only makes sense that we should fatten ourselves by feasting on His word.

Preparation and the Number 3

We see why preparation is important, but why the number 3? What is the significance of 3 days?

The number 3 embodies the completeness of the Godhead — the Holy Trinity of The Father, Son and Holy

Spirit. It also represents the totality of mankind of body, mind and spirit. The number 3 is the spiritual number of completeness, perfection, divine fullness and fulfillment. It also illustrates preparation. This is important because before a process of change and transformation can begin, a completed time of preparation must be fulfilled.

Before Jesus was arrested, He went to the Garden of Gethsemane to pray. He took Peter, James and John — the three closest to Him. He agonized in the garden three times in prayer. He prayed so intensely that He was sweating blood (Luke 22:44). These three prayers are indicative of a time of preparation. Jesus was preparing for what was about to take place. He was preparing for His death. He was preparing for the completion of His role as the promised Messiah who would give His life on the cross for the forgiveness of sin, the destruction of death and the grave, and the salvation of all who receive Him. The completion of this came with His resurrection from the grave that occurred 3 days and 3 nights after his death.

Mentioning the importance of the number three and its relation to Jesus' death, brings us to story of Jonah.

"For as Jonah was in the belly of the great fish for three days and three nights, so will the Son of Man be in the heart of the earth for three days and three nights (Matthew 12:40, NLT)."

The story of Jonah and his three days in the belly of the fish points to Jesus. It highlights the number three as the number of preparation. This biblical account also accurately depicts how a period of preparation comes before consecration. Let's briefly examine the story found in Jonah chapters 1-3.

In the first chapter, The LORD gave Jonah specific instructions to go to Nineveh and announce His judgment against the people because of their wickedness. Jonah disobediently ran from The LORD and these instructions. He went down to the port of Joppa and boarded a ship headed for Tarshish in order to escape. The LORD caused a terrible storm to arise that tossed the ship about violently. The ship's crew soon discovered that the storm was a result of Jonah's disobedience to God. Eventually, they have no choice and decide to toss him overboard. The LORD arranged for a big fish to swallow Jonah and keep him in its belly for three days and three nights. He spent this entire time praying and crying out to The LORD.

Here we see Jonah in the secret place with God, praying and calling out for salvation.

> *"And he said, 'I cried out to the LORD because of my affliction, And He answered me. Out of the belly of Sheol I cried and You heard my voice.'"* ~Jonah 2:2

Jonah cried out from Sheol. *Sheol* in Hebrew refers to the grave or the place of the dead (Psalm 88:3-5). It also represents a falling apart, a place of dissipating (Job 7:9) and being turned to dust (Job 17:16). This is the chrysalis. The chrysalis is a place of death for the caterpillar. It's where the caterpillar goes to die, to fall apart, to vanish and dissipate. This holds true for the spiritual chrysalis we enter during consecration. We fast and pray while in this place of death. We cry out to The LORD as we die to self in the secret place. We cry out for salvation. We cry out to be saved. Crying out to be saved and set apart for divine use is the purpose of consecration.

After the three days and nights of preparation were complete, The LORD had the fish spit Jonah out onto dry land. The LORD asked Jonah again to go to Nineveh—a city so large it took 3 days to see it all—and deliver His message to the people. This time Jonah was obedient. When Jonah told the King of The LORD's plan to destroy the city, the

King humbled himself. He stepped down from his throne and removed his royal robes. He wrapped himself in burlap, sat on a heap of ash and declared a fast.

What we see here is the king of Nineveh obediently entering into a time of consecration. The removal of his royal robes and stepping down from the throne shows him humbling himself. He then wraps himself in burlap. This action can be likened to the caterpillar entering its chrysalis. It can be likened to the believer wrapping herself up in the secret place.

The king then sits on a heap of ashes. This is a picture of sacrifice. He submitted to the word and authority of the one true God, surrendered all and now is ready and willing to give himself as a living sacrifice. This perfect coming together of truth, intimacy, submission, sacrifice, surrender, obedience and faith is consecration. The king did this in hopes that God would "change his mind and hold back his fierce anger" from destroying the people of Nineveh (Jonah 3:9). When God saw this, He showed mercy on the people of Nineveh and did not carry out His plan to destroy them. It is also important to note that the King's act of consecration came after Jonah's three days of preparation.

Preparation before fasting is vital. So for the next three days, be a caterpillar! Gorge on spiritual leaves! Eat, drink and feast on the written word of God. Get fat and full! Get the word deep inside so that it can be quickened and used at the proper time.

Eat up! Our time in the Chrysalis is drawing near!

Here are a few scriptures regarding feasting and quickening to get your appetites rolling.

NOTE In whatever area you are seeking breakthrough, research the scriptures and feast on what the Bible says regarding that area of your life. The following verses are simply suggestions. Appetizers, so to speak. Make this fast personal to you and your current circumstances.

Feasting and Quickening Scriptures:

"On the last day, that great day of the feast, Jesus stood and cried out, saying, "If anyone thirsts, let him come to Me and drink. "He who believes in Me, as the Scripture has said, out of his heart will flow rivers of living water."
John 7:37-38 NKJV

"So He humbled you, allowed you to hunger, and fed you with manna which you did not know nor did your fathers know, that He might make you know that man shall not live by bread alone; but man lives by every word that proceeds from the mouth of the LORD."
Deuteronomy 8:3 NKJV

"But He answered and said, "It is written, 'Man shall not live by bread alone, but by every word that proceeds from the mouth of God.' ""
Matthew 4:4 NKJV

"Your words were found, and I ate them, And Your word was to me the joy and rejoicing of my heart; For I am called by Your name, O LORD God of hosts."
Jeremiah 15:16 NKJV

"Then I took the little book out of the angel's hand and ate it, and it was as sweet as honey in my mouth. But when I had eaten it, my stomach became bitter. And he said to me, "You must prophesy again about many peoples, nations, tongues, and kings.""
Revelation 10:10-11 NKJV

"I am afflicted very much: quicken me, O Lord, according unto thy word."
Psalms 119:107 KJV

"It is the Spirit who gives life; the flesh profits nothing. The words that I speak to you are spirit, and they are life."
John 6:63 NKJV

"But if the Spirit of Him who raised Jesus from the dead dwells in you, He who raised Christ from the dead will also give life to your mortal bodies through His Spirit who dwells in you."
Romans 8:11 NKJV

Fasting Reminders and Suggestions:

1. Fasting is defined as the abstaining from all food or certain types of food. Fasting can be held 24 hours around the clock or for certain time periods during the day. For example, one can enter into a water only fast from 6:00 AM to 6:00 PM.

2. Fasting is not giving up social media, television shows, your favorite video game, etc. That is actually called **self-denial**. Self-denial in conjunction with fasting is highly recommended and beneficial. Remember to guard your heart and mind. Anything that pulls your attention away from what God is saying should be avoided during this fast.

3. There are different types of fasts. There are **absolute fasts,** where you consume no food or water; **water only** fasts, where you consume only water; **liquid only** fasts, where you consume liquids only and no solid foods. There are even vegetable only fasts. Seek God on how your fast should look. I often do liquids only with a small evening meal of lean fish and steamed vegetables or liquids only around the clock. Again, seek God's instruction for you.

4. Consider any dietary or medical restrictions that may prevent you from fasting and make adjustments accordingly. Remember: no one has ever been instructed by a doctor to eat fried foods and sweets. So if you have medical condition that will not allow for drastic changes in your diet, then consider fasting sweets, sodas and unhealthy fats. Make a pledge to avoid unhealthy eating options. Everyone can fast safely in one way or another. If you are currently under a physician's care or have any questions or concerns, seek the advice of your medical provider before you begin.
5. Keep a Bible or Bible app handy at all times.
6. Invest in a journal and take full advantage of the writing space provided in this book. Record the revelations, instructions and downloads you receive. Journal each day. Several times a day if necessary. Expect to hear from God.
7. Begin and end the fast with Holy Communion. Take in the gifts of His body and blood as a gesture of your deep love, adoration and commitment to Christ.
8. ***You may have a designated place for prayer in your home, and that's wonderful. But please remember, the secret place can be in your prayer

closet, in your car, at work or in a busy grocery store. The secret place is a heart posture. It is a place deep within you. You carry it with you always. Learn to move into the secret place with The Father even when there are crowds of people around.

***Remember, no one's fasting journey looks the same. You will be taken from faith to faith and glory to glory. Your next level depends on which level you are on currently. Your experience in the secret place is between you and The Father.

Prayer for Preparation:

Heavenly Father, in the name of Jesus, touch my heart and my mind as I prepare myself to enter into the secret place with you. Consecration is a process that requires me to crucify my flesh. This will not feel good, Father. Help me to focus on your word that lives in me during the uncomfortable times. I cannot live by bread alone. And I cannot get through the tough times without your word in my spirit. Feed me the goodness of Your word. Plant it deep in my spirit and allow it to nourish me. In Jesus' Mighty Name, Amen.

Declarations for Preparation:

I declare I am hungry for the word of God.

I declare I cannot live by bread alone but by every word that comes from the mouth of God.

I declare I hear the voice of God and the voice of another I will not follow.

I declare I well prepared for the fast time ahead.

I declare that I am committed to transformation, breakthrough and new beginnings in my life.

I declare I will SEEK, WORSHIP and EAT during this time of preparation. The groundwork will be laid.

BEFORE WE BEGIN

Pause. Breathe. Take a moment right here and consider the amazing journey on which you are preparing to embark. The next 11 days (3 of preparation, 8 of fasting) will be life changing for you. No longer will you be a caterpillar in the spirit crawling about aimlessly. No longer will you feel the desire to fly higher but are unable to because something is holding your wings captive. The lid above you is about to be lifted! The ceiling is about to be broken! You are about to experience transformation like never before! And when you break out of your chrysalis, you will simultaneously experience breakthrough and a new beginning!

Take the time to truly consider your reason for fasting. Are you praying and fasting for increased faith? For peace and purity? Perhaps, unity, wisdom and insight. Are you fasting to receive divine direction for your next steps in your career, personal life, finances or ministry? Are you fasting for the divine strategy to break every chain of bondage, opposition and resistance? Whatever area of life in which you are experiencing a plateau, pray and fast for the keys to breakthrough.

Consider your dreams. Consider what God has spoken over you. What do you aspire to be? What is God calling you to become? What resources do you need to carry out this call? Have you heard His call but feel unsure regarding the details? What is He calling you to birth? What is He wanting to do in and through you?

Have you been feeling stuck and weighted down? Have fear and doubt been holding you back? You cannot carry out the vision God has for your life if you are filled with confusion. If you are crawling around feeling downtrodden and despondent, with no hope for the future, then how can you fly into the purposes He has for your life?

Everything you need for your transformation and breakthrough is on the inside of you. Allow God to stir it up. Let go and let Him show you.

Let me leave you with this: You may be clear on your calling, yet, need breakthrough regarding its fulfillment. Or perhaps you are uncertain about what your exact calling is. The fact that you have invested in this book tells me that you have, at least, heard His voice in some capacity. It tells me you know there is something more He wants from you.

Participating in this fast is your response. Participating in this fast is the next right thing, because consecration is what must come after you hear His call. During this period of consecration, you will receive revelation, clarity and instruction. And once your consecration is complete, God will commission you. He will send you out with specific instructions to complete for His divine purposes. But it has to happen in this order:

Called, Consecrated, Commissioned.

Your new beginning awaits. All you need are your wings! Let's get started!

Preparation Day 1

SEEK:

Look for The LORD in your situation. Seek Him in prayer. What is He saying? Speak your heart to Him and allow Him time to respond. Ask questions and set goals? Record it here.

_____

_____

_____

_____

_____

_____

_____

_____

_____

_____

_____

_____

_____

_____

_____

_____

WORSHIP:

Position your heart and mind. Worship Jehovah God in spirit and in truth. Sing songs and play worship music. Use this space to pen a beautiful display of worship to Him.

EAT:

It's time to feast on the word! What scriptures has God highlighted for your specific situation? Record and reflect on them here.

_____

_____

_____

_____

_____

_____

_____

_____

_____

_____

_____

_____

_____

_____

_____

_____

_____

_____

_____

Preparation Day 2

SEEK:

Look for The LORD in your situation. Seek Him in prayer. What is He saying? Speak your heart to Him and allow Him time to respond. Ask questions and set goals? Record it here.

WORSHIP:

Position your heart and mind. Worship Jehovah God in spirit and in truth. Sing songs and play worship music. Use this space to pen a beautiful display of worship to Him.

EAT:

It's time to feast on the word! What scriptures has God highlighted for your specific situation? Record and reflect on them here.

Preparation Day 3

SEEK:

Look for The LORD in your situation. Seek Him in prayer. What is He saying? Speak your heart to Him and allow Him time to respond. Ask questions and set goals? Record it here.

WORSHIP:

Position your heart and mind. Worship Jehovah God in spirit and in truth. Sing songs and play worship music. Use this space to pen a beautiful display of worship to Him.

EAT:

It's time to feast on the word! What scriptures has God highlighted for your specific situation? Record and reflect on them here.

_____
_____
_____
_____
_____
_____
_____
_____
_____
_____
_____
_____
_____
_____
_____
_____
_____
_____
_____

Fast Day One

DEDICATION

Welcome to the Chrysalis! This is the first of Eight Days of Prayer and Fasting for Transformation, Breakthrough and New Beginnings! I am confident you will be blessed.

Today's focus: **Dedication**!

The definition of dedication, along with its synonyms, can be broken up into three parts. According to the Oxford English Dictionary, dedication is defined as:

1. "The quality of being dedicated or committed to a task or purpose." Synonymous with commitment, persistence, perseverance, devotion, loyalty and allegiance.
2. "The action of dedicating a church or other building." Synonymous with blessing, consecration and sanctification.
3. "The words with which a book or other artistic work is dedicated." Synonymous with inscription, address and message.

All three of these definitions and their synonyms apply to this experience. Let's be a reflection of this 3-part definition today. Let's devote this day and this fast to three things:

1. Let us dedicate and commit ourselves to the process of being transformed. Let us persevere in our quest to completely die to self. Let us persistently seek The Lord's voice regarding our callings. Let us pledge loyalty and allegiance to The LORD that His will may be made perfect in us.

2. Let us recognize that our bodies are houses. We are temples of The LORD. Let us dedicate our houses to God. Let us bless and consecrate our hearts and minds and humbly invite The LORD into our tabernacles. Let us give way to the process of our temples being rebuilt, refashioned and repurposed. Let us recognize that are we are spiritual houses designed for His good use.

3. Let us remember that we are an artistic work created by The Father. Let us dedicate ourselves to Him by inscribing His Name and His Word on our hearts and minds.

A wonderful way to begin this time of consecration is by taking in the gifts of Holy Communion. This is not for the purposes of being ritualistic or religious. But, instead, should be a prophetic display and symbolic gesture of love and appreciation for Christ and the ultimate gift of salvation that was given to all mankind through His death and resurrection. Taking in the gifts of communion shows your commitment to Jehovah, Our Father; Jesus Christ, Our Savior and Holy Spirit, Our Comforter. This is a wonderful way to show your dedication to this time of consecration.

Jesus said, "It is written, 'Man shall not live by bread alone, but by every word that proceeds out of the mouth of God (Matthew 4:4)." As we begin this fast, let us spend this day dedicating and committing ourselves to The Father, His instructions and revelations, and to the transformation that will take place over the next eight days. Let us dedicate ourselves to being transformed by the renewing of our minds (Romans 12:2).

"However, anything specially set apart for the Lord – whether a person, an animal, or family property – must never be sold or bought back. Anything devoted in this way has been set apart as holy, and it belongs to the Lord." ~Leviticus 27:28, NLT

It is important to recognize that this transformation cannot take place if we are exposed. As part of the dedication process, The Father is wrapping and covering us.

"He shall cover you with His feathers, and under His wings you shall take refuge; His truth shall be your shield and buckler."
~Psalm 91:4 NKJV

The Hebrew word *sakak* means "to cover, hedge in, protect, or shut up (enclose)" where the enemy cannot reach you. Just as a caterpillar enters into its protective chrysalis, this, too, is a day of being wrapped up in His covering. What an amazing exchange! When we dedicate and give ourselves over to Him, He gives us His covering and protection.

Consecration is big deal. It's a crucifying of the flesh. Thus, we need Our Heavenly Father to be in the midst of this with us. We need Him to be at the center of this transition. We are literally embarking upon a move from one state of being to the next. We need His presence while this evolution takes place. We need His covering.

In Isaiah 4:5, God gave the Israelites His covering as they were transitioning. His presence manifested as a cloud by day and a fire by night. As they traveled, God placed a canopy of His Glory over them. He will do the same for us. His word shows us that He will be with us in times of change. Whenever we are positioning ourselves to grow spiritually and move to higher levels in Him, there He is in the midst.

"God is in the midst of her, she shall not be moved; God shall help her, just at the break of dawn."

~Psalm 46:5, NKJV

"The LORD your God in your midst, The Mighty One, will save; He will rejoice over you with gladness, He will quiet you with His love, He will rejoice over you with singing."

~Zephaniah 3:17, NKJV

    I pray you experience the protective covering of His Mighty Wings as you walk through this day dedicating yourself to the transformation process that must occur before the outset of your new beginning.

Prayer for Dedication:

Heavenly Father, I enter Your gates with Thanksgiving. I enter Your courts with Praise! I humbly approach Your throne and ask Your forgiveness for any sins I have committed, both knowingly and unknowingly. I meekly lie down at Your feet. I am reaching out and grabbing a hold of Your Mighty hand as I enter into this fast with You. I devote, dedicate and commit the next 8 days to You and to the work You must do in me. I willingly and humbly enter into this Chrysalis experience. I am committed to the process of being melted down, refined and reassembled. Wrap me up in Your Mighty Wings. Cover and protect me as You transform, renew and cleanse me. I pledge my allegiance to You and to this 8 days of consecration. I dedicate myself to becoming all You created and designed me to be. I mark myself as belonging to You alone. I thank You for calling me. Make me holy and righteous in Your sight. I am Your vessel. Take me from caterpillar to butterfly. Help me breakthrough every barrier. Give me wings to fly into my new beginning.

In Jesus' Mighty Name, Amen.

<u>Declarations for Dedication:</u>

I declare the next 8 days are dedicated to my consecration.

I declare that the word of The LORD nourishes me.

I declare I am focused, committed and devoted to this process.

I declare I am humbly and willfully entering the chrysalis — the secret place with The LORD.

I declare my allegiance and loyalty to my Heavenly Father.

I declare that He is covering and enveloping me with His mighty wings just as a caterpillar is encased and protected in its chrysalis.

I declare a canopy of Glory is over me.

I declare The LORD is with me in the midst.

I declare I have dedicated myself to being wholly submitted, sacrificed and surrendered.

I declare that I am being consecrated, cleansed and set apart.

I declare that I belong to My Heavenly Father. His name and His word are inscribed upon my heart.

Significant Scriptures:

CHRYSALIS JOURNAL MOMENT

Revelation and Reflections

What is The Father saying to you? What are you experiencing?

_____

_____

_____

_____

_____

_____

_____

_____

_____

_____

_____

_____

_____

_____

_____

_____

_____

_____

_____

Fast Day Two

DISINTEGRATION AND ILLUMINATION

Welcome to Day Two of our 8-Day fast. Today gets a little harder—physically, emotionally and spiritually. Today is when the heat is introduced. Trust The Father. The heat is good and necessary. Hold His hand and focus on His word, and you will indeed make it through.

Today's focus: **Disintegration and Illumination!**

Disintegration, as defined by the Oxford English Dictionary, is "the process of losing cohesion or strength; the process of coming to pieces; the breaking down of something into small particles or into its constituent elements."

According to the same source, illumination is defined as "lighting or light; clarification; revelation; spiritual or intellectual enlightenment."

After the caterpillar enters into its chrysalis, it is melted down into a soup. It is disintegrated and literally broken down into a liquid. After this melting takes place, every biological component that is not beneficial or necessary for its rebirthing as a butterfly is highlighted, revealed and illuminated.

Interestingly, the same is true for precious metals like gold and silver. Before these metals are sold, they go through a process of refinement in the refiner's fire. The gold or silver is taken through a melting process. It is disintegrated so that its impurities can be illuminated. These impurities reveal themselves by rising to the surface.

We, too, must be willing to allow The Father to melt us down, to dissolve us and disintegrate us into all our basic parts that He may then illuminate that which is not beneficial. When God melts us down, we are able to "see" every component...the good worth keeping as well as those things that are toxic and impure.

These impurities are stumbling blocks...stones...the stony bits and hardened places of our hearts. If not addressed, they will build up over time causing a dam...a blockage that will stop the flow of rivers of living waters.

God's word says, "out of [your] belly shall flow rivers of living waters (John 7:38)." If we wish to be a part of these rivers of living waters, we must be able to continue the flow. Not one of us can change the entire world alone, but we can cause a ripple. We can be a ripple that carries with it a ripple effect. We can allow God's glory to flow on, in and through us. We can allow God to work through us to affect positive and righteous changes in the lives of others. If the work we do for the Kingdom touches the lives of a handful of people, and, in turn, they each go on to touch the lives of a handful of people—and this cycle continues—then what you have created is a ripple effect. And this ripple effect will continue the flow of the rivers of living waters.

As you are melted down today, God will illuminate and highlight every loose rock that could clump together to form a dam. Allow Holy Spirit to shed light on every stony part of your heart that could impede the flow of the rivers of living waters. Let Holy Spirit show you any traces of unresolved hurt, bitterness, rejection and offense. Are you being burdened by people whom you thought you had forgiven? Situations you thought you had resolved and overcome? That must be handed over to The Father. Unforgiveness will cause the flow of living waters to cease. Repent and surrender it all to Him.

God's Kingdom needs its people to allow these rivers to flow freely from their bellies. This flow will advance the

Kingdom of God and be a source of energy for the Body of Christ.

When God melts you down into all your basic parts—when He disintegrates you—you are able to see every component. Everything that is unnecessary and toxic is illuminated. He shows you every stumbling block. He shows you every little stone and every stony bit of your heart. These tiny, loose stones build up over time if not addressed. They form a dam—a blockage—and the flowing waters will flow no more. The river will become stagnant and lifeless.

When we starve, deprive and crucify our flesh through prayer and fasting, Our Heavenly Father begins to reveal things. He shows us the ugly, impure and hardened parts of ourselves that we would otherwise deny or overlook. He shows us our yucky bits.

What impurities, stumbling blocks and yucky bits is God revealing to you?

_____
_____
_____
_____
_____

Knowing is half the battle. Knowing where your issues lie gives you the upper hand. It gives you specific focus in prayer. Now, you can repent, ask for forgiveness and turn it over to God.

"I will raise my fist against you. I will melt you down and skim off your slag. I will remove all your impurities."
Isaiah 1:25, NLT

"Fire tests the purity of silver and gold, but the Lord tests the heart."

~Proverbs 17:3, NLT

"So they tied them up and threw them into the furnace, fully dressed in their pants, turbans, robes, and other garments. And because the king, in his anger, had demanded such a hot fire in the furnace, the flames killed the soldiers as they threw the three men in. So Shadrach, Meshach, and Abednego, securely tied, fell into the roaring flames. But suddenly, Nebuchadnezzar jumped up in amazement and exclaimed to his advisers, 'Didn't we tie up three men and throw them into the furnace?' 'Yes, Your Majesty, we certainly did,' they replied. 'Look!' Nebuchadnezzar shouted. 'I see four men, unbound, walking around in the fire unharmed! And the fourth looks like a god!'"

~Daniel 3:21-25

Prayer for Disintegration and Illumination

On this day, Father, thank you for disintegrating me. Thank you for melting me down. Thank you for the refiner's fire that is meant to test the purity of my heart and mind. I submit and surrender to Your fire. I willingly sacrifice this flesh in Your fire. As I am melted down, thank you LORD for illuminating the toxins and impurities in my life. Thank you for highlighting the areas of my heart that need to be cleansed and purified. Thank You for illuminating that which I no longer need and that which can hurt or hinder me. There are certain elements the caterpillar no longer needs to become and function as a butterfly. Thank you for showing me what I no longer need as I prepare for my next season. In Jesus' name, Amen.

Declarations for Disintegration and Illumination

I declare I am being disintegrated by the power of The Almighty God.

I declare that I am being melted down by The Refiner's fire.

I declare that God is with me in furnace. He is with me in the chrysalis. He is with me as I am being pulled apart.

I declare that every unclean thing in me is being illuminated and brought to my attention.

I declare every toxin is being revealed.

I declare these rocky and stony parts will not become a dam designed to interrupt the flow of rivers of living waters.

I declare these impurities will not become stumbling blocks.

I declare that rivers of living water flow from my belly.

I declare I am a Ripple Maker!

I declare I will cause a ripple effect of righteousness in the rivers of living waters.

Significant Scriptures:

CHRYSALIS JOURNAL MOMENT

Revelation and Reflections

What is The Father saying to you? What are you experiencing?

_____
_____
_____
_____
_____
_____
_____
_____
_____
_____
_____
_____
_____
_____
_____
_____
_____
_____
_____

Fast Day Three

ELIMINATION

Welcome to Day Three of our 8-day fast. Your discomfort has likely intensified. If so, that's a good sign…it's working. Times of prayer and fasting are not intended to feel good. After all, you are going through a process of death—a dying to self.

Today's Focus: **Elimination**!

Elimination is defined as "the complete removal or destruction of something; the expulsion of waste matter from the body."

After the caterpillar is melted down, the biological material that is not necessary for its future as a butterfly is digested and eliminated, leaving only the components that will come together to create a beautiful new creature.

Now that The Father has melted you down and highlighted that which is harmful and impure, it is time to focus on your Elimination process. It is now time to rid your body of the filth that was exposed.

All the impurities that were highlighted and illuminated yesterday need to be eliminated today. All the toxic emotions and memories that were remaining must be flushed out. As the residual toxins are being released spiritually and emotionally, you may even experience a release of impurities physically. You may find yourself going to the restroom more than usual today.

You may also find yourself having imaginary conversations or creating fictional scenarios in your head in an effort to purge your mind of past hurts and wounds. This is healthy. Get it all out. Use the privacy of the secret place to say the things that are on your heart and mind. Cry out to God. Shout. Stomp. Be honest with Him regarding these emotions and thoughts. Get these toxins out of your system. Release it to Him and let it all go, once and for all.

Having toxins eliminated from your body, soul and spirit is liberating. It's freedom. But a great deal of honesty with yourself as well as trust in the Holy Spirit is required.

As we move through this day, allow and trust Holy Spirit to guide you in eliminating every toxic thought, feeling, emotion, memory, cycle and situation. Allow Holy Spirit to rid your body, soul and spirit of every destructive impurity.

"Therefore, get rid of all ill will and all deceit, pretense, envy, and slander. Instead, like a newborn baby, desire the pure milk of the word. Nourished by it, you will grow into salvation, since you have tasted that the Lord is good. Now you are coming to him as to a living stone. Even though this stone was rejected by humans, from God's perspective it is chosen, valuable."

~1 Peter 2:1-4, CEB

"Jacob said to his household and to everyone who was with him, 'Get rid of the foreign gods you have with you. Clean yourselves and change your clothes.'"
~Genesis 35:2, CEB

"Therefore if the Son makes you free, you shall be free indeed."
~John 8:36, NKJV

"So then, brethren, we are not children of the bondwoman but of the free."
~Galatians 4:31, NKJV

I pray Our Lord and Savior Jesus Christ be with you during this day of elimination that you may rid yourself from any remnants of impurity and truly be free.

Prayer for Elimination

Father, in the name of Jesus, I humbly approach You and ask You to meet me right here where I am. I am covered in impurities. Remove the muck and scum that has been illuminated. Eliminate every unclean thing from my life, my heart and my mind. Remove all unnecessary burdens, hurts and wounds. The pain I've experienced in life has left me with toxins that can never benefit me. I don't want these toxins in my life anymore, Father. Rid me of these harmful things. Take it all away from me. Remove every trace of it from my life. I surrender it all to You.

In Jesus' Mighty Name, Amen.

Declarations for Elimination

I declare every impurity is eliminated from life.

I declare The LORD is scraping off all the scum that has risen to the surface.

I declare that I am free from all past hurts, pain and wounds.

I declare that I no longer carry around toxins that cannot benefit me.

I declare I am rid of all uncleanliness.

I declare that I am chosen and valuable in the eyes of God.

I declare He is cleansing me and changing my clothes.

I declare I no longer have a caterpillar mentality.

I declare I have only the substance and character traits of a Kingdom butterfly.

Significant Scriptures:

CHRYSALIS JOURNAL MOMENT

Revelation and Reflections

What is The Father saying to you? What are you experiencing?

_____

_____

_____

_____

_____

_____

_____

_____

_____

_____

_____

_____

_____

_____

_____

_____

_____

_____

_____

_____

Fast Day Four

PURIFICATION

Today is Day Four of our 8-Day Fast. And the fire is being turned up again.

Today's focus: **Purification**!

Purification, as defined by the Oxford English Dictionary, is "the removal of contaminants from something; the process of making something spiritually or ceremonially clean."

When God creates good changes in us, He has to solidify them. As He shapes and molds us, those changes must be cured and perfected for them to be long-lasting. Any remaining impurities must be heated and burned away.

When a potter creates a new vessel, that vessel must go into a large fiery furnace called a kiln. The heat of this specialized oven is designed to cure, solidify and purify the vessel.

Jehovah is our Divine Potter, and we are His pottery. He must refine, solidify and purify us. As His vessels, we must undergo purification by fire in order to be tested, perfected and readied for good use.

Challenging situations will likely present themselves today. These situations are for the purpose of testing, solidifying and perfecting the good traits in you...the good traits that remain after the illumination and elimination processes.

The purification of a vessel has to occur before a new thing can be placed in it or before it can be used for a new purpose. The heat must be turned up to ensure that that vessel is perfect for good use.

Menstruation is another example of purification. The lining of the womb must be shed in order to prepare it for the implantation of the fertilized egg. This is true in the natural and in the spiritual. Before a new thing can be planted in us and eventually birthed, we must be purified and perfected.

> *"Therefore, since we have these promises, dear friends, let us purify ourselves from everything that contaminates body and spirit, perfecting holiness out of reverence for God."*
> *~2 Corinthians 7:1, NIV*

"I will bring the one –third through the fire, will refine them as silver is refined, and test them as gold is tested. They will call on My name, And I will answer them. I will say, 'This is My people';

And each one will say, 'The LORD is my God.' "
~Zechariah 13:9, NKJV

"But He knows the way that I take; When He has tested me, I shall come forth as gold."
~Job 23:10, NKJV

"that the genuineness of your faith, being much more precious than gold that perishes, though it is tested by fire, may be found to praise, honor, and glory at the revelation of Jesus Christ,"
~I Peter 1:7, NKJV

"For You, O God, have tested us; You have refined us as silver is refined." ~Psalm 66:10, NKJV

Thank you Father for the fire, tests and trials that purify and perfect our holiness. In Jesus' Name. Amen

Prayer for Purification:

Father God, purify me. Purify me in the fire. Light your flames beneath me and burn away every impurity. Solidify the good changes you have made in me. Create in me a clean heart and renew in me a steadfast spirit. Then allow my heart and mind to be put through the refiner's fire for purification and perfection. Place me in the kiln and cure me. Thank You Father for perfecting everything that concerns me. The heat doesn't feel good, but it is for my good. Thank You for every test and trial that you have allowed to purify and perfect my holiness.

In the name of Jesus, Amen.

Declarations for Purification

I declare I am purified and refined in the Refiner's fire.

I declare every test is purifying me.

I declare every trial is purifying me.

I declare every good change that has been created in me is being refined and locked in place.

I declare I am being purified for holiness.

I declare I am being made spiritually clean.

I declare I am a purified vessel.

Significant Scriptures:

CHRYSALIS JOURNAL MOMENT

Revelation and Reflections

What is The Father saying to you? What are you experiencing?

_____

_____

_____

_____

_____

_____

_____

_____

_____

_____

_____

_____

_____

_____

_____

_____

_____

_____

Fast Day Five

REVELATION

Welcome to Day Five of our 8-day fast. Expect to receive divine and prophetic revelation today followed by confirmation.

Today's focus: **Revelation**!

The Oxford English Dictionary defines revelation as "a surprising and previously unknown fact, especially one that is made known in a dramatic way; the making known of something that was previously secret or unknown; the divine or supernatural disclosure to humans of something relating to human existence or the world."

Isaiah 59:2 NKJV says, "But your iniquities have separated you from your God; And your sins have hidden His face from you, So that He will not hear." Impure and sinful hearts will prevent us from seeing Our Father's face. But because of purification, we are cleansed of our iniquities and covered under the blood of Jesus Christ.

> *"But now in Christ Jesus you who once were far off have been brought near by the blood of Christ."*
> *Ephesians 2:13 NKJV*

After being purified, we can be certain that God will begin to reveal His heart and mind to us...even His Marvelous Face! Revelation is a gift, a blessing that is received after purification.

"Blessed are the pure in heart: for they shall see God."

~Matthew 5:8

Receiving Divine Revelation is a sign that you are blessed and that The Father Himself is sharing His heart and mind with you.

"Jesus answered and said to him, "Blessed are you, Simon Bar-Jonah, for flesh and blood has not revealed this to you, but My Father who is in heaven."
~Matthew 16:17 NKJV

The first time I did this fast, I received a powerful prophetic revelation on this Day Five. On this particular morning, I heard a voice that was not my own singing within me. It sang:

"I hear a trembling, coming down, down, down...Heaven is calling, can't you hear the sound, sound, sound."

Immediately following, I had an impression about those believers whose spiritual roots are firmly planted in the ground and that those souls who are lost better get found. Right away, I asked, *"God, what are you saying? Give me scripture for this."* Immediately, Isaiah 46:12 dropped in my spirit. I read verses 12-14 in the NKJV. They read as follows:

"Listen to Me, you stubborn-hearted, who are far from righteousness: I bring My righteousness near, it shall not be far off; My salvation shall not linger. And I will place salvation in Zion, For Israel My glory."

Then God led me to Isaiah 13:13, NKJV. It reads:

"Therefore I will shake the heavens, and the earth will move out of her place, In the wrath of the LORD of hosts and in the day of His fierce anger."

This was so powerful, and I was in amazement. I decided to read all of Isaiah chapter 13. As I finished, God downloaded this prophetic revelation into my spirit. My hands began to write the words He was speaking to me:

"A Divine Shaking. God is bringing about a Divine Shaking that will shake loose debris. Anything not rooted in The Rock, in The Word — His Son Christ Jesus — He will shake it loose from the earth. He will cause this shaking to remove the hands of the unrighteous from that which belongs to the righteous. And those institutions that have been taken over by the ungodly will be given unto those who are holy! Those who carry the very presence of God

will be lifted as those who do the works of evil will be shaken loose! There will be a Divine Shaking! Can you not hear it! Can you not feel the tremors!

Wicked people turn from your ways! Run to the Only True God! Those who are lost, get found! Get free! Get rooted! Plant your roots deeply and firmly into the ground...the Rock! The earth is coming under a Divine Shaking! The trembles, tremors and quaking will shake off that which is dead, fruitless, useless and vile! Just as the wind blows away the chaff, God will shake off the unnecessary. He will shake off that which cannot be used! That which is not securely rooted.

Like a child doing artwork shakes off the excess glitter that did not stick, God will shake off those that are not planted...those that are not rooted...those that are not securely fastened down in The Word!

Let the Divine Shaking go forth! Shake, Shake, Shake! It is so!"

Immediately after, I had a vision of a prophetic image. I knew I was to draw the image and release it along with this word. I wanted to be obedient, but before I could release that which was so intense and powerful, I needed confirmation. So I asked God for it. Later that same evening, I tuned in to a Facebook Live video about prayers that activate Glory Carriers by Prophetess Michelle McClain-Walters. And lo and behold, it was exact confirmation of what The LORD had given me. She talked about the "Divine Shaking" with such passion, power and strength. She used those exact words…"A Divine Shaking." And because of God's confirmation, I had the faith, courage and confidence necessary to release the prophetic image and His word.

God's voice didn't stop there on that day. He also had a word for me regarding my role in The Kingdom. He revealed to me the importance of my spiritual womb and the process of purification that is essential for reproduction. He spoke specifically to me about giving birth. He revealed that I have a fertile womb and am capable of bringing forth life in the spirit. That word changed everything for me. That word was breakthrough. Knowing that The LORD's desire is to birth goodness for His people through me humbles me. But it also gives me the confidence to move forward in all He instructs me to do. And not confidence in myself, but confidence in Him and His word.

Because of my Day Five testimony, I have faith that The LORD will reveal Himself to you. I encourage you to expect revelation today. It may not be a big display. It may not be a word meant for public consumption. But, it may be a revelation designed specifically for you and your life situation. It may be the revelation that results in your transformation, freedom and breakthrough. It may be the revelation that ushers you into your new beginning.

Continue to sit with Him here in the secret place of the chrysalis. No matter how revelation shows up, I am confident it will bring clarity to your calling and instructions and answers regarding your next.

There's a private place reserved for the lovers of God, where they sit near him and receive the revelation-secrets of his promises."

~Psalm 25:14, TPT

As you move forward on this Day of Revelation, may Holy Spirit reveal to you the deep things of The Father (Examine 1 Corinthians 2:10). In Jesus' Mighty Name, Amen!

Prayer for Revelation

Heavenly Father, in the name of Jesus, I thank You for showing me your heart today. Thank You for sharing what is on Your mind concerning your plans for me. Thank You for seeing me as one who loves You and for reserving a seat just for me in the secret place. Thank you for opening Your heart and sharing precious mysteries. Open my spiritual senses and sharpen my discernment. Help me to be confident in Your voice when I hear it. Send confirmation of Your word. Don't let me miss it. In Jesus' Mighty Name, Amen.

Declarations for Revelation

I declare I have been invited into the secret place with the Most High.

I declare He has reserved a place for me.

I declare God shares His heart with me.

I declare God shares His mind with me.

I declare God shares divine secrets, plans and strategies with me.

I declare I know the Voice of The LORD God Almighty.

I declare He will confirm His word to me.

I declare I will not miss what He is saying.

I declare The Father calls me blessed.

I declare my heart and mind reflect the heart and mind of The Father.

I declare He can trust me with His revelations.

I declare I will cover every revelation in prayer and act on it in the way Jehovah instructs.

Significant Scriptures:

CHRYSALIS JOURNAL MOMENT

Revelation and Reflections

What is The Father saying to you? What are you experiencing?

Fast Day Six

REPLICATION

Welcome to Day Six of our 8-Day fast.

Today's focus: **Replication**!

"I am the vine, you are the branches. He who abides in Me, and I in him, bears much fruit; for without Me you can do nothing."

~John 15:5, NKJV

The goal for believers should be to die to self so that Christ might live in and be seen in us. Fasting and praying for consecration is one means of attaining this goal (Galatians 2:20). When flesh is crucified and consecrated, Replication (Divine Replication) occurs.

Yesterday was a day of Revelation. A day of God sharing His secrets. Once God reveals His heart and mind to us, then He can replicate it in us. Replication can only come after Revelation.

In the Oxford English Dictionary, replication is defined as "the action of copying or reproducing something; the process by which genetic material or a living organism gives rise to a copy of itself." In molecular biology, DNA

Replication is the biological process of producing two identical replicas of DNA from one original DNA molecule.

We have the DNA of the father. We have the DNA of Christ. And the word says we are made in the image of God. When sin pulled mankind out of perfection, it took a perfect man to die for us. Christ came down from glory and became the sacrificial Lamb that would take on the sins of the world. We are covered under His blood once we choose Him as our Lord and Savior. But receiving salvation is only the beginning.

As we continue our walk with God, our desire should be to walk in holiness, to answer the calls placed on our lives, to advance the Kingdom and to move to new, higher and deeper levels in the things of God. New levels and callings require consecration. As consecration is achieved, Christ is replicated in us. As we are cleansed and set apart, Christ's DNA, actions, thoughts, words, heart, feelings, and desires are reproduced in us.

In the chrysalis, the DNA of the caterpillar is the same as that of the butterfly, yet they look completely different. We have always had the DNA of Christ, because we were made in His image. But a dying to self must occur and a transformation must take place in order for us to look, act and think like Christ. The same is true for the caterpillar and butterfly. Cells are replicated and a change must take place in order for the caterpillar to look, act and think like the butterfly. They are completely different, yet share the same DNA.

It is here during the Replication stage of the fast that consecration occurs. At this point, we should have fully surrendered and allowed Christ to completely abide in us.

Congratulations, you are a new creation!

"Therefore, if anyone is in Christ, he is a new creation; old things have passed away; behold, all things have become new."
2 Corinthians 5:17

Prayer for Replication

Jehovah Heavenly Father,

I pray that Christ be replicated in me. I ask that my mind, heart, words, thoughts and actions be that of Christ. From the top of my head to the bottom of my feet, make me an exact replica of your Son, Jesus Christ. It is no longer I who lives, but Christ who dwells in me. Take every old thing away, and make me a new creation.

In Jesus' Mighty Name, Amen.

Declarations for Replication

I declare I am an exact replica of Christ.

I declare it is no longer I who lives but Christ who lives in me.

I declare I have the mind of Christ.

I declare I have the heart of Christ.

I declare I am a new creation in Christ Jesus.

I declare I have the DNA of the Father.

I declare I am consecrated.

I declare I am set apart for God's divine purposes.

I declare I am a branch.

I declare I am connected to the vine.

I declare I abide in Christ.

I declare Christ abides in me.

I declare I bear good fruit.

Significant Scriptures:

CHRYSALIS JOURNAL MOMENT

Revelation and Reflections

What is The Father saying to you? What are you experiencing?

_____

_____

_____

_____

_____

_____

_____

_____

_____

_____

_____

_____

_____

_____

_____

_____

_____

_____

_____

Fast Day Seven

SANCTIFICATION

Welcome to Day Seven of our 8-Day fast. You may be wondering why there's a Day Seven if consecration was achieved yesterday. We're not finished, yet! There is more to be established.

Let me explain. Consider this:

After the caterpillar has been completely transformed into a butterfly, its chrysalis becomes transparent. The new creation pushes its way out of the soft shell that was once its hard, protective covering. This is Breakthrough. After breakthrough has taken place, the butterfly hangs upside down while it begins to unfold and expand its wet, newly formed wings. It must rest in this position. Before it can take flight, its wings need to air out and dry. But they also need one more vital element…blood. Yes, the butterfly's wings need to be pumped full with blood.

This is true for you and me, as well. Today you have broken through, and now you need blood. The precious blood of Jesus Christ. It is through the blood of Jesus and the Spirit of God that we are sanctified.

Today's Focus: **Sanctification!**

To be sanctified is to be set apart and marked as holy. There is a difference between consecration and sanctification. Consecration is something WE do. It is a time of crucifying our flesh, surrendering, separating ourselves from sin and cleansing ourselves. Sanctification, on the other hand, is a divine act. It is something GOD does.

Let's compare 1 Peter 1:2 in the NLT and the NKJV versions:

"God the Father knew you and CHOSE you long ago, and HIS SPIRIT HAS MADE YOU HOLY. As a result, you have obeyed him and have been cleansed by the blood of Jesus Christ. May God give you more and more grace and peace."

1 Peter 1:2 NLT

"elect according to the foreknowledge of God the Father, IN SANCTIFICATION OF THE SPIRIT, for obedience and sprinkling of the blood of Jesus Christ: Grace to you and peace be multiplied."

1 Peter 1:2 NKJV

When God chooses you to be set apart, it is His Spirit and the blood of Jesus that sanctifies and makes you Holy.

"But you are a CHOSEN generation, a royal priesthood, a HOLY nation, His own special people, that you may proclaim the praises of Him who called you out of darkness into His marvelous light;"
I Peter 2:9 NKJV

Consecration precedes Sanctification. Once we have consecrated ourselves, the Father can now Sanctify us — Set us apart and call us Holy for His specific use.

"Therefore if anyone CLEANSES himself from the latter, he will be a vessel for honor, SANCTIFIED and useful for the Master, prepared for every good work."
II Timothy 2:21 NKJV

<u>*Prayer for Sanctification*</u>

Heavenly Father,

Thank You for choosing me, for sanctifying me and marking me as holy. Thank You for setting me apart and designating me for specific Kingdom use. Thank You for multiplying the grace and peace that will help me carry out my assignments.

In Jesus' name, Amen.

Declarations for Sanctification

I declare I have been transformed and made new.

I declare I have experienced breakthrough.

I declare I have been sanctified by my Heavenly Father.

I declare I have been made holy by His Spirit.

I declare I have been washed clean in the blood of my Savior Jesus Christ.

I declare I am chosen.

I declare I am royal.

I declare I am a sanctified vessel of honor.

I declare I am designed for The Father's use.

Significant Scriptures:

CHRYSALIS JOURNAL MOMENT

Revelation and Reflections

What is The Father saying to you? What are you experiencing?

Fast Day Eight

ELEVATION

Today is the final day of our 8-Day fast! We made it! Today's Focus: **Elevation**!

This eight day fast has been one of transformation, breakthrough and new beginnings. Just like a caterpillar undergoes changes to become a butterfly, we went through the processes of being encased in a chrysalis, melted down, refined, cleansed, purified and refashioned. We have successfully broken through and allowed our wings to be filled with the blood.

Today, it is time to fly! Today is a day of Elevation! The day we are lifted up. The day we take flight in our new understandings of what God has for us in this season, who He has chosen us to be and how He intends to use us. We have been commissioned for every good work.

> *"No longer do I call you servants, for a servant does not know what his master is doing; but I have called you friends, for all things that I heard from My Father I have made known to you."*
> *John 15:15 NKJV*

Over the last 8 days, God has made Himself known to us. He has revealed His heart and mind to us. In doing so, we have been elevated! We are transformed and new! We are no longer servants, but friends. We are friends of Christ Jesus and through Him all things of The Father are revealed. We have been Elevated and commissioned.

Butterfly, you have your flight plan. Now Fly!

Prayer for Elevation

Jehovah Heavenly Father, I approach you with a thankful heart. Thank You for guiding me through this eight day journey of fasting and praying. Thank You for spending time with me in the secret place. Thank You for Your transforming touch. Although it was my obedience that led me to this time in the chrysalis, it was Your Spirit that showed up and gave me wings. Thank you for my breakthrough and my new beginning in You. Thank You, Father, for elevating me and commissioning me to carry out Your good works. I thank You that I am no longer a servant but a friend to Your Son, Christ Jesus. Guide me as I take flight. Elevate me from glory to glory and faith to faith.

In the Mighty Name of Jesus, Amen!

Declarations for Elevation

I declare I have been Elevated.

I declare I am flying into my New Beginning.

I declare the Father has placed a grace on my wings to carry out the assignments He has placed before me.

I declare all Glory and Honor belong to Jehovah!

Significant Scriptures:

CHRYSALIS JOURNAL MOMENT

Revelation and Reflections

What is The Father saying to you? What are you experiencing?

FINAL THOUGHTS

"We have become his poetry, a re-created people that will fulfill the destiny he has given each of us, for we are joined to Jesus, the Anointed One. Even before we were born, God planned in advance our destiny and the good works we would do to fulfill it."
~Ephesians 2:10, TPT

I want to let you in on a secret. You are a beautiful creation. God's masterpiece. His poetry. He has always seen you this way. He sees you as the being He created you to become. He sees past old hurts and wounds. He sees beyond past faults and character flaws. He sees outside of our limitations and gazes in amazement at the beauty He placed in you.

While mankind easily views you through the judgmental and tainted lenses of your transgressions and mistakes, God sees who He has called and created you to become.

Mankind sees the dirty worm—the greedy caterpillar.

God sees the butterfly.

The flawed vision of man may perceive you as the worm in Jonah Chapter 4 that ate through the plant causing it to shrivel and die, but God sees you as His creation. And He wants you to see that, too.

I have another secret to share. You're not finished with your chrysalis…Keep it close. Unlike the caterpillar that can only enter its chrysalis once, we have the ability and privilege to enter into the chrysalis experience as many times as needed. We are always changing and evolving, always growing and moving from one level to the next. Each time we are called to another level, realm or dimension, we should consecrate ourselves. Each time a new layer or element of our calling is revealed, we should enter into a chrysalis experience with the LORD.

Because we go from faith to faith and glory to glory, our consecration prepares us to be commissioned for what's next. But sometimes this upward movement is met with resistance. Sometimes, there's a lid. Sometimes you need to be transformed in order to receive breakthrough and a new beginning. Sometimes you need…

Consecration in the Chrysalis

www.ingramcontent.com/pod-product-compliance
Lightning Source LLC
Chambersburg PA
CBHW060538100426
42743CB00009B/1562